Bluebell

BLUEBELL

George Perry

The authorized
biography of Margaret Kelly,
founder of the legendary
Bluebell Girls

PAVILION
MICHAEL JOSEPH

This edition published in Great Britain in 1987 by
Pavilion Books Limited
196 Shaftesbury Avenue, London WC2H 8JL
in association with Michael Joseph Limited
27 Wrights Lane, Kensington, London W8 5TZ

First published in 1986

Designed by Lawrence Edwards and Madeline Serre

The majority of photographs in this book have been
taken from Miss Bluebell's private albums and
scrapbooks, but those specifically provided by other
sources are:
AFP Photo 136, 145; BBC Hulton Picture Library 37;
George Clarkson 33, 35; Fox Photos Ltd 152; Keystone
Press Agency Ltd 100, 137, 139; 19° Regiment du
Génie, Besançon 109; George Perry 220, 221, 222, 224;
Rex Features Ltd 191, 197; The Sunday Times/David
Montgomery 15; Ulstein Bilderdienst 31.

Perry, George
    Bluebell.
    1. Kelly, Margaret.   2. Dancers–Biography
    1. Title
    793.3'2'0924   GV1785.K4

ISBN 0–907516–75–0 (Hbk)
ISBN 1–85145–033–5 (Pbk)

Printed and bound in Great Britain by
Butler & Tanner Limited, Frome, Somerset.
Typeset by PCS Typesetting, Frome, Somerset.

Contents

Acknowledgements

To write a book on Miss Bluebell is a pleasurable task, not least for the willing co-operation and enthusiasm of the subject herself, who was prepared to devote day after day of her very busy life to the task. It all began in 1981 when Peter Baker telephoned me at *The Sunday Times* and invited me to visit him at Worthing to discuss the possibility of a magazine article on the Bluebell phenomenon. Shortly after seeing him I decided to go to Paris to meet her, taking with me the photographer David Montgomery. The result was published as a cover story in *The Sunday Times Magazine* of 23rd August 1981.

Normally journalism is ephemeral — one topic quickly succeeds another and there is rarely an after-life for an article. The Bluebell feature, enhanced by David Montgomery's brilliant pictures, and a selection of memorabilia from her archives, attracted considerable attention, largely because it was the first time that one of the so-called "quality" British newspapers had devoted its pages to an examination of this remarkable woman and her work.

Richard Bates, a television producer with years of experience in the industry and the begetter of many outstanding programmes, proposed that a biography be written and simultaneously a drama series based on her extraordinary life be mounted. He and publisher Colin Webb of Pavilion Books shortly afterwards met Miss Bluebell and were quickly convinced that such an interesting joint venture could be achieved. Between them they made the creation of this book possible.

There were many others besides Bluebell herself who made the task enjoyable, and if the cries of colleagues are to be taken seriously, enviable. In particular thanks are due to Donn Arden in Las Vegas; Douglas Scott at the Lido in Paris; Caroline Taylor and her successor as Bluebell's secretary, Michele Wormser; Moira Armstrong, the director, and her production staff of the BBC *Bluebell*, particularly Sophie Neville; the scriptwriter Paul Wheeler; many Bluebells current and past, but especially Katherine Dunne, Tanya Spencer, Nicola Harvey and Miranda Coe; Vincent Page for part of the picture research; Lawrence Edwards for his inspired book design skills; Colin Webb and his staff at Pavilion Books, Vivien Bowler in particular; Pat White, my patient agent; and my wife Frances, who encouraged, supported and assisted in the preparation of the book. I am very grateful to everyone mentioned here, and to all those others who helped, and for whom space is insufficient to list individually. It was fun.

Barnes, London, September 1985

Foreword
by Miss Bluebell

In my lifetime, I don't think I could possibly estimate the number of times that friends, relations, even perfect strangers have suggested to me that the story of my life should be written. Being of a positive nature, I have never been against any of these suggestions, and I have even seen the beginning of certain projects, an outline here or a first chapter there. These projects, however, have always fallen apart, due, I feel, to procrastination, or perhaps a lack of perseverance.

An autobiography was out of the question. I don't think that I have ever read one that I considered completely honest. Good qualities always seem to be exaggerated, and any bad ones so white-washed that the author ends up being a character beyond belief. Being Irish born, I certainly am aware of the blarney I would be capable of inventing.

In 1981, an article about me appeared in the magazine of *The Sunday Times*, London. It was while reading this article with its succinct phrasing, its agreeable pace, and its pleasant humour that it crossed my mind that the author, George Perry, would be the ideal person to write the book that you are about to read.

I have always been an enthusiastic collector. Photographs, playbills, publicity, and eschewing further alliteration, contracts, musical arrangements and tape recordings have always been dutifully packed away in a cupboard or closet wherever I was living at the time. When George Perry and I began talking about collaborating on a book, I know he was amazed at the wealth of material that I brought out to show him. To make things easier, I had all of this material taken out of the large heavy envelopes and cardboard boxes, arranged chronologically by date and year, and everything pasted into extra large scrapbooks. George and I spent many hours looking through these scrapbooks, where a picture or an article would bring back a memory of a story of that period which I would relate to him. I am very thankful that I have a good memory so that I could accurately recall the names of people and places.

In spite of the fact that I have a twenty-four hour a day job (for the captains of my groups throughout the world can telephone me at any time), I manage to stay in very close contact with my family. Patrick, my eldest son, is also the most serious. When my husband, Marcel, was killed in a terribly unfortunate automobile accident, Patrick became the Head of the family, a responsibility he still manages with altruistic determination. At an early age, Patrick developed an ability to disconnect his hearing and block out all conversation going on around him, leaving himself able to pursue his own train of thought. Quite a trick until a question would be directed to him personally when he would have to plug himself in again and ask for the question to be repeated. He used to drive me wild with this habit! Patrick now lives in Las Vegas, Nevada, with his wife Patricia, a wonderful girl, and a beautifully trained "danseuse étoile".

My second son Francis, lives here in Paris with his wife and family. Francis was known as the perennial student. Indeed, because of his studies of foreign languages and international law, he was still taking examinations at the age of twenty-eight! It all paid off well though, for he now has an excellent position with the French Government in the Ministry of Agriculture.

My son Jean Paul, married one of my Bluebell Girls, and they went to settle in London. They had a beautiful baby girl, but their marriage seemed to flounder, and I am sorry to say, finally ended in a divorce. Loquacious is the word for Jean Paul. Of all my children, he is the one who inherited the Irish gift-of-gab. As one of his co-workers told me one day, "Jean Paul could talk the hind legs off a donkey". He lives here in Paris, and he is at present connected with the Méridien Hotels chain.

I have left my daughter Florence last, but she is definitely not last in my heart. Florence and I are, in fact, quite alike, although she has never been interested in anything theatrical. Florence now lives in perfect harmony in Las Vegas with her ever so likeable husband, Mel. One of my favourite anecdotes about Florence occurred one early evening when we were both going to a cocktail reception, I believe at the British Embassy. We were both decked out in cocktail dresses, perfumed and jewelled for the occasion. In the taxi, before reaching the Embassy, Florence leaned toward me and said as one would say to a child: "Now remember, Mummy, if we have more than one gin and tonic, we do not discuss religion, we do not discuss politics, and we do not discuss our war experiences."

I hope that no one will find me presumptuous for writing the prologue to my own life's story. I am doing so hoping to make myself seem more real to those who will be reading the book. Mine has been a wonderful life. Full of some bad times, but by far, many many more marvellous ones. I hope you will enjoy this book, and so, enough repetitious phrases . . . read on!

BLUEBELL
Paris, 12th September 1985

1 Nuits De Paris

AVENUE DES CHAMPS-ELYSEES is arguably the most famous street in the world. Its noble width far exceeds that of Fifth Avenue, Piccadilly, Wilshire Boulevard and the Kurfurstendamm. Le Notre's carriage ride became the Elysian fields in 1709, and later in the eighteenth century it was extended as far as the Seine at the Pont de Neuilly. But before the 1830s the avenue west of the Rond Point des Champs-Elysées, where it ascends to the great Napoleonic monument, the Arc de Triomphe, was a nondescript collection of suburban buildings, punctuated by an occasional mansion. The broad street was used by stall holders to peddle fruit and vegetables to travellers into the French capital city; it was a neighbourhood where it was unwise to be out after dark. Places of entertainment — cafés, circuses, restaurants — were opened up to cater for racegoers returning from Longchamps. The installation of the new gaslit street lamps vanquished the more blatant footpads. During the era of the Second Empire the area was transformed as the business axis of Paris moved westwards; both sides of the thoroughfare were now lined with imposing, if monotonous buildings.

The twentieth century brought with it cars, autobuses and the Métro. The width of the street gave plenty of opportunities for the setting-up of the

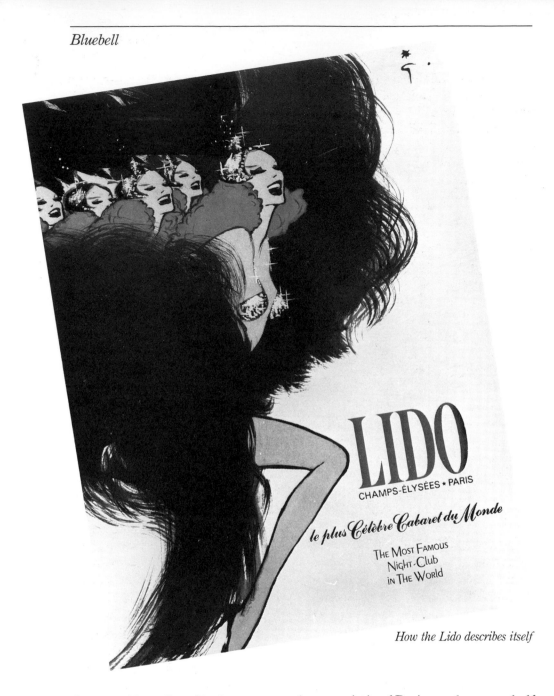

How the Lido describes itself

famous sidewalk cafés that were so characteristic of Paris — where one half of the population could sip aperitifs, and ogle the other half on their promenade. Tourists were encouraged to believe that it was here that the heartbeat of this great city was most keenly felt. On 14th July each year it becomes the most important processional route in the whole of France. The victory parade which took place on 'le quatorze juillet' of 1919, following the ending of the First World War, led to the interment of the Unknown Soldier, directly beneath the vault of the great Arch of Triumph in the following year, and the kindling of the eternal flame, which was to flicker constantly over the grave from 1923 onwards, even during the sad days after 1940 when Nazi Germany occupied the city. It was from this same point that General de Gaulle began his pedestrian pilgrimage to the cathedral of Notre-Dame, on 26th August 1944, the day following the Germans' formal surrender of the city. After his death in 1970, which was marked by a silent march along the Champs-Elysées, the Place d'Etoile became the Place Charles de Gaulle, but Parisians, much in the way that New Yorkers can never quite bring themselves to call Sixth Avenue 'The Avenue of the Americas', go on using the old name.

Paris, unlike London with its West End, or New York with the Broadway theatre district, does not have a single concentrated centre of night life, where the theatres, cinemas, night clubs and cabarets can be found in close proximity to each other. Instead, there are several such areas — Pigalle, Opéra, Montmartre, Montparnasse, St Germain, the Latin Quarter, for example. The most celebrated music hall in the world, the Folies Bergère, is in the Rue Richer, an obscure back street near the Opéra. The imposing stretch of the Champs-Elysées between the Rond Point and L'Etoile, however, became renowned for its places of entertainment, which were sandwiched between restaurants and cafés. The authorities, intending to preserve the elegance of the thoroughfare, decreed that only white neon signs would be permitted to advertise such attractions, and for many generations the Avenue has been a magnet for innocent pleasure seekers.

Nowadays, there are perhaps too many fast food establishments jostling the traditional cafés, and the aroma of burgers mingles with the petrol fumes from the hundreds of cars that jam up the gravel strips on either side of the central roadway, which is a nightmare for anyone attempting to cross on foot. When the traffic lights at the Avenue George V intersection turn green each driver seems to imagine that he is at Le Mans. On the south-east corner of this busy junction is the famous restaurant, Fouquet's; across the Champs-Elysées on the opposite side, to the north, and next to a Mercedes car showroom, is the Normandie cinema, with billboards advertising the current attractions on its three screens, and, counterpointing them, a modest neon display. For this is the home, since 1977, of the establishment which, with no false modesty, describes itself as '*Le plus Célèbre Cabaret du Monde*'. The long entrance lobby, in the form of a carpeted corridor from the street, is shared with cinemas, and bisected by a central rail. The new Lido was carved out of what was once the stalls area of one of the biggest pre-war cinemas in Paris, where stage shows for a while accompanied the latest film releases. In France, as elsewhere, the fashion for huge picture palaces faded, and the premises were more satisfactorily divided to maximize their entertainment value, and to make better use of one of the best sites in the city.

Around dusk on a summer's evening there is an air of heady anticipation

11

Panache—*the 1985 show at the Lido*

around this narrow street frontage. The birdsong in the young trees abates as the high pressure sodium street lights snap on. Cars jostle for the last available inch of parking space, the underground garages being already full, and their drivers risk fines and tows as well as impeding the paths of patient pedestrians. Tour buses unload eager groups of sober-suited Japanese holidaymakers, who form an orderly line to enter this legendary cathedral of delectation. Customers are claiming their reservations; the ones who left it too late are turned away, because for nearly every night of the year, save for a few slack weeks in January, the Lido is solidly booked out. Every day of the year it functions, even at Christmas, and it is only when a new show is in its final stages of preparation that the Lido bars it doors to the public.

What is it, then, that makes this place such a magnet for visitors? The food is excellent, and dinner, including champagne, starts at 370F. There is a dance floor where couples still dance in the old-fashioned way, clutching each other as they whirl to the orchestra's rhythm. People make a point of dressing up to go to the Lido — the men usually wear suits, and invariably

ties, the women dresses and high heels. The jeans and tee-shirts of more casual establishments are scarcely *de rigueur* here. But then, a visit to the Lido is an occasion, an event to be relished to the full. And the highpoint of the evening begins at 10.30, when the tables nearest the dance floor begin to sink, and a stage miraculously emerges. From that moment there follows a lavish, spectacular, vivid show, which for two-and-a-half hours assaults the senses with its attention-grabbing music, colour, movement, light and energy.

The Lido show can accommodate waterfalls, ice rinks, a Czar's Palace, a jungle with real elephants, even an exploding airship. The sets are dazzling and ingenious, and form themselves mechanically before the audience with precise timing, creating bridges, ramps, staircases, podia for the dancers. The brilliant lighting effects add to the magic of the performance, which moves at an incredible pace, honed by constant practice into an inexorable smoothness. There are individual acts between the most lavish of the set-pieces — jugglers, illusionists, acrobats, dog-trainers, mind readers, strong men — but no star turns, because it is the show itself that is the star.

And, of course, the dancers. The show is full of beautiful girls, costumed in sequins, silks, feathers, frills and flesh-toned fishnet tights. Some wear little more than rhinestoned G-strings, others are clad head to foot in shimmering gowns. For all of them there are countless costume changes, and scarcely a second to ease the pressure of performance. Each of them is immensely tall and bears herself, even when almost naked, like a princess, graciously bestowing on the audience a sparkling, constant smile. There are male dancers as well — agile young men who first appear in blue-sequinned jackets, snow-white trousers, scarlet waistcoats and matching bowlers. They, too, are tall, but alongside the girls, particularly when the Junoesque beauties are wearing mountainous headdresses, they seem overshadowed.

It is for such spectacular entertainment that the audience has gathered. For those visitors from overseas it is the highpoint of their trip to Paris. For the French it is a pilgrimage to one of their most cherished national institutions. For the Parisians it is a celebration. The Lido is timeless Paris. While the show that is staged in the mid-1980s will use the most up-to-date, state-of-the-art electronic technology to make its effects, the tradition to which it belongs goes back more than a century, when the French capital first acquired its reputation for joyous, irrepressible frivolity and constant gaiety.

It would be strange, then, to discover that these astonishing dancing girls, so synonymous with this aspect of Paris, are, for the most part, not French. But that is indeed the case. At least 80 per cent of them come from Britain, a land that has no place of entertainment remotely comparable with the Lido. How could the squalid little strip clubs of Soho or the raucous working men's clubs in the industrial heartland of England be regarded in the same context as such jewels of the Parisian night as the Lido, the Moulin Rouge or the Folies Bergère?

Behind the dancers there is, inevitably, a powerful personality who shapes and welds them into a cohesive force, who instils into these girls the qualities that set them apart from the others. The Bluebell Girls, as they are known, at the Lido are the elite of dancers in show business. They are like a crack regiment of Guards — their average height is an Amazonic 5ft 11in, and any girl shorter than 5ft 9in is not even considered for recruitment. But it is more than mere inches that makes a Bluebell Girl. Each is selected very carefully for her personality as well as for her dancing skills.

They take their name from the extraordinary Miss Bluebell. Every night this remarkable woman is backstage at the Lido by 8.30, ensconced in a tiny dressing room bearing the number '13' on the door, which serves as her office. There she will pass on instructions to the captains of the Bluebell Girls and the Kelly Boys, her two groups there, and talk to any members who have problems, as well as deal with the dozens of minor details constantly calling for attention. Later she will watch each of the two

Miss Bluebell with two of her dancers

performances that night, the first at 10.30, and the second, slightly shorter version at 1.30 a.m. Both will receive her hawk-like attention, with little getting past her. It will be nearly four in the morning before she will take her taxi home.

It is part of a world to which she has belonged for almost sixty years, with more than fifty of them in charge of her own dance troupe. Anyone meeting her for the first time is amazed that someone who radiates so much dynamic energy is a septuagenarian. She still has a trim dancer's figure, and her eyes are bright and clear, her hair silvery but cut short and neat. Perhaps most surprisingly she is well below the minimum height of one of her dancers, being around 5ft 7in, which still puts her well above the average.

I first met Miss Bluebell in the early summer of 1981, having gone to Paris to write a magazine article about her which was to anticipate the fiftieth anniversary of the founding of the Bluebell Girls. Her world is a corner of show business which has received less than its fair share of attention, in spite of its immense and continuing popularity. The glitter and the excitement lure not only the patrons, but hundreds of would-be performers, and there is never a shortage of potential Bluebells, attracted by the high reputation of the troupe and the woman who runs them. Her very first words to me after I had been shown to her centrally-placed table at the Lido an hour before curtain-up, were: 'I'm a character, you know!' And as in later meetings details of her remarkable life story emerged it became clear that there was not a hint of exaggeration in her assertion, merely her forthright acknowledgement of her unique position at the top of her calling.

2   Beginnings

WHETHER OR NOT BLUEBELL has greasepaint in her veins cannot be determined; she has no idea if any of her forebears were connected with the theatre or the other performing arts. The reason is that she has no idea who they were. What is known is that on 24th June 1912, at the Rotunda Hospital in Parnell Street, Dublin, a baby girl was born to a woman called Margaret O'Brien. The father's name was given as James Kelly. It is not certain whether or not they were married, but later the priest who prepared the baptismal certificate offered a strong suggestion that they were, perhaps a kindness in an age when illegitimacy was accorded a stigma that is not customary in today's social climate. The little girl was named Margaret Kelly.

Some three weeks after her birth a priest visited a family which consisted of three unmarried sisters and their brother, all adults, who were living in O'Connell Street (a principal Dublin thoroughfare which before the emergence of the Irish Free State was known as Sackville Street). He asked if the eldest of the sisters, Mary Murphy, would be prepared to look after the baby for three months or so. He told them a white lie — that the parents were going abroad, and could not take a tiny infant with them. The brother,

Peter Murphy, was not at all happy with the priest's request in view of the fact that his sisters were all spinsters, but they over-ruled him, and so he decided to leave the house permanently.

The Murphys were poor, but not uneducated. Both their parents had been teachers, but had died leaving nothing for their children. Mary Murphy worked at home as a dressmaker, while the others went out to work. Consequently, it fell to her to take care of the baby. In spite of the fact that there were no husbands the priest had chosen the Murphys because they were a deeply religious family, attending Mass every day.

Nearly seventy years later, Miss Bluebell, née Margaret Kelly, went back to Dublin, and visited the Rotunda Hospital. The Matron told her that although substantial modernization had taken place in recent years the old maternity wing was still intact, and after checking hospital records she was even able to identify the bed in which the birth would probably have occurred, although it had been long since retired from active service. Bluebell never came into contact with her parents, and she grew up completely uninterested in tracing them. They had, she claimed, never done anything for her, and she did not even feel curious about them. However, on the same trip to Dublin she made an attempt to find their address as given on the baptismal record. It had vanished many years previously. She even went into a newsagent's shop near the probable location, and asked the man behind the counter if he knew of any people called Kelly who lived in the vicinity. Alas, the surname Kelly is to the Irish as Smith is to the English, and his answer was scarcely helpful.

The little girl's mother had left three months' money for Mary Murphy to look after the child, but was never seen again.

Bluebell recalled that in spite of the comparative poverty of her infant home there was no neglect, and that she always had proper baby clothes, and even a snow-white bassinet. It is her theory that Mary Murphy became so fond of her that she would have been greatly distressed if her real mother had shown up to claim her, and did absolutely nothing to encourge such a possibility. Meanwhile, Mary Murphy's two sisters at last found themselves husbands, and left the small house.

A Dublin general practitioner, one Dr O'Connor, was the person who unwittingly bestowed on young Margaret Kelly the name she would use for the rest of her life, and by which the world would come to know her. Entranced by the infant's clear blue eyes, her most prominent facial feature, he said: 'You're my little Bluebell!' As the child was thin and sickly the doctor was in fairly constant attendance. Her legs were match-like, too weak to support her body, and for a while it was feared that she would never walk. It was not until she was well past her third birthday that she first took a few unaided, tottering steps. Standards of nutrition and hygiene were far less advanced then than today, and in Ireland there was a high rate of infant mortality. But the determination and devotion of Mary Murphy was a powerful force, and she willed the child through to better health. The struggle was a difficult one because money was scarce, and hard-earned. Sometimes, when there was no work available to her as a dressmaker, Mary Murphy would pay a child minder two shillings and sixpence to look after Bluebell while she went out to scrub floors all day to earn perhaps four shillings and sixpence.

Meanwhile, following the Easter uprising of 1916, Ireland's protracted political agonies erupted into violence, with bloody fighting in the streets of Dublin. Mary Murphy, facing both penury and danger, made the decision to leave her unhappy homeland, and attempt to find work in England. With the last vestige of her savings she bought ferry tickets for Bluebell and herself, and sailed across the Irish Sea to the great port of Liverpool, where already many thousands of Irish migrants had found a satisfactory new home, including the rest of her family.

Liverpool, standing on the wide estuary of the River Mersey, facing Wallasey and Birkenhead in Cheshire on the opposite shore, and adjacent to the South Lancashire hinterland, with to the east the large industrial city of Manchester to which it was linked by a deep canal big enough to take sea-going ships, was at that time Britain's most important seaport after London. The great Atlantic liners then still sailed from Liverpool rather than Southampton, and the miles of docks lining the Mersey thrived with Lancashire cotton goods, machine tools, coal, the factory products of the industrial north being exported to the far reaches of the then flourishing British Empire, while wheat from Canada, cotton from India, tobacco from America passed across the wharves in the opposite direction. Liverpool had that special vitality often found in a major port, a warmth and outgoingness that befitted its mercantile tradition, and there were to be found there lively local communities where the native-born Liverpudlians were supplemented by newcomers bringing fresh notions from the world beyond. Liverpool has contributed far more than its fair share to the entertainment industry. Some of Britain's greatest comedians — among them Tommy Handley, Arthur Askey, Ken Dodd, Ted Ray — came from there, and in the Sixties a plethora of celebrated pop groups, led by the most famous of them all, the Beatles. Both John Lennon and Paul McCartney had Liverpool–Irish origins. When a Liverpool newspaper recently featured Miss Bluebell in an article, they added that she came from the town of the Beatles. Her comment was that they had got it wrong — the Beatles came from her town, as she antedated them by a considerable number of years.

It was to the West Derby district that Mary Murphy gravitated, where she already had a number of relations. Today West Derby is a populous eastern suburb of the city, forming the Liverpool 12 postal area, and the houses are newer and spaced more widely apart than in the dense inner parts, but are nevertheless still contained within the outer ring road, the M57, which nowadays marks Liverpool's physical limits. In the earlier

The teenage Bluebell: 'Does your mother know you're out?'

years of the century it was a village some way beyond the urban spread, with an old parish church, a group of small shops, and a straggling series of tiny houses. It owed its development to the tram system, a municipal network which, for a few pence, could transport the inhabitants to the city centre aboard smooth-running cars that hissed along gleaming rails under the overhead trolley wire.

Mary Murphy and the five-year-old Bluebell moved into a two-roomed house in Deysbrook Lane. Separating the front door from the street was a yard or two of front garden, but on the inside there was no hallway — the street door opened directly into the principal room, which had a fireplace, and in an alcove at the back, a sink with a cold tap. There was no electricity, or even gas, and lighting and cooking were dependent on oil. The stairs to the upper storey led straight out of the room, and the floor above consisted of a bedroom containing Mary's bed and Bluebell's cot. There was no indoor sanitation. The outdoor privy was shared with an identical house behind, and because they were not even connected with main sewerage a septic tank had to be cleared out twice yearly by the local authority. For the people in the other two-roomed house of the pair, across the communal entry, life was even harder, for they had two children.

Every Friday a ritual visit was paid to the public bathhouse, where hot water was available in scalding quantities. Few houses at that time in the industrial north of England had bathrooms, and the municipalities provided facilities where for a few pence their customers could soak themselves in gigantic bathtubs, then towel themselves vigorously on the wooden duckboards inside their cubicles. Clothes could also be washed at these places, first stewed in big copper vats, then beaten and wrung by hand on serrated washboards. It was possible to maintain cleanliness and a good appearance at the cost of hard work, and Bluebell's 'Auntie Mary' anxiously asserted her pride in the way she made sure her tiny charge was turned out.

The house, 48 Deysbrook Lane, has long vanished. On its approximate site stands a neat council house, part of a spacious estate built in the Sixties. The living room where Bluebell spent so many of her formative years has been superseded by a trimly mown lawn forming part of the front garden of the redeveloped house, and Deysbrook Lane itself, lined with its parked Fiestas, Metros and Cavaliers, is scarcely recognizable from how it looked some sixty-five years ago.

Mary Murphy found herself a job as a ward maid at a local hospital, for which she was paid £1 for a six-day week, with only Saturdays off. The rent for the cottage was five shillings a week, which left fifteen shillings, the balance of her weekly income, for them to live on. The diet for the most part consisted of eggs, potatoes and boiled onions with butter. Meat was rarely available, except when Mary took Bluebell to a weekend lunch at the home of one of her married sisters.

Bluebell's first school was Leyfield Convent, which she began attending at the age of five. As Mary had to leave for work shortly after seven in the morning, she made sure that Bluebell was dressed and ready to be collected by an older child, with whom she then walked to the school, which was a mile away. She would carry with her some bread and jam sandwiches, which she would eat halfway through the day. When she returned she would have to wait until 7.30 in the evening for Mary Murphy to get back from the hospital before she could have her supper.

The convent catered mainly for boarders, but took a score or so of local children with limited means as day pupils. The nuns were firm, but not unduly strict, and coped with Bluebell's energetic high spirits with patient good humour. When she played in the street with other children in the neighbourhood she was always known as Bluebell, but at the convent the mother superior insisted that she should only be addressed as Margaret. 'No pet names here, thank you very much!' she would rasp at anyone who dared to transgress her rule.

Because there was no one to look after her if she became ill, colds and flu were frequent childhood ailments, and Bluebell was frequently put in the Alder Hey Children's Hospital, which was only a few hundred yards from the convent. She also spent several weeks at a sanatorium in Formby, along the coast to the north of Liverpool, to recover from a bout of scarlet fever. But in spite of her frailties she was a lively child, a tomboy who was always bursting to get out of school so that she could run and play in the street. She was also very frequently in trouble for talking in class, instead of getting on with her lessons, and after one particularly serious admonishment Mary Murphy was summoned to the school to discuss her work performance. One of the subjects in which her marks were giving concern was French. Impatiently Bluebell complained to her guardian: 'Why should I learn French? I'm never likely to go to France!'

There was also the sacred pastime of childhood, the stealing of apples from the branches. In the Twenties there were extensive orchards at the end of Deysbrook Lane, which at the appropriate time of the year formed a magnet for young children. From the end of the day at school until well after 7 p.m., when Mary Murphy was due to return from the hospital, Bluebell was at liberty to roam the streets and to get up to mischief. But on one occasion the farmer caught her red-handed up a tree, abandoned by her accomplices, who had fled at his approach. He let her go with a stern warning, and so effective was it that she stayed well away from the trees following it. It was not the farmer who bothered her so much as the fierce dog accompanying him.

Such activities were bound to take a toll on her clothes. Mary Murphy nurtured a belief that it was better to go hungry than to be seen publicly in a state of dishevelment, and so she was at pains to ensure that Bluebell was generally spruced-up and tidy, and that her dress was clean, crisp and well-ironed. She was a deft needlewoman, and was obliged to become an expert at repairing the ravages of childish over-activity.

There was concern for Bluebell's frail legs, and one of the doctors who was in regular attendance took the view that she would have to engage in exercise of some sort to give them strength. In the days before it became compulsory for schools to provide physical education many made no attempt to do so, and Leyfield Convent was one such. So self-help was necessary. The idea emerged that dancing might be the answer, and a better way of building up the slender, tiny body than more straightforward exercises. Mary Murphy was greatly attracted to the ballet, and was constantly borrowing library books on the subject — almost as though she herself was a frustrated ballerina.

There was a woman in the city of Liverpool who styled herself Madame Cummings, and ran a dancing school. At the age of eight Bluebell began going to her classes on Saturday mornings, Mary Murphy using up part of her precious day off work to take her into town on one of the green and

Harlequin themes were popular for Twenties dance numbers

cream corporation trams. The fee for the lessons was two shillings and sixpence – half-a-crown – for each attendance. The premises are no longer to be found, having been built over some years ago by the encroaching University of Liverpool, but they were close to Myrtle Street, in the central district of the city. After a year or two Bluebell was able to make the tram journey on her own, first walking a mile from her home to the West Derby tram terminus, and then, after reaching the stop in the city, ascending the steep hill leading to the dancing school. The mothers, she recalled, were kept well clear of the class itself, and had to wait in a room outside, where they could catch occasional glimpses of the activities within by craning over the top of a partition. Most of the other little girls in the class came from far more privileged backgrounds than that of Bluebell, and were attending for social reasons rather than for the therapeutic value of dance, or from a desire to go on the stage.

Bluebell, however, found that she had a natural ability and could learn steps quickly. The nuns at Leyfield Convent, far from censuring her new-found outlet for her obvious energy, gave their wholehearted encouragement, and even allowed her to leave school early on some days when classes clashed. In return Bluebell staged special displays of dancing in order to entertain the orphans who were boarded at the school during the Christmas holidays.

But her irrepressible character was seen, as she grew older, to represent a hindrance to the convent's sense of order. On one occasion a girl was foolish enough to boast that her panama hat, which had cost all of three guineas, was indestructible, and Bluebell, taking up the challenge, swiftly proved the statement to be an exaggeration. The outraged mother swooped on the school, demanding compensation, which the mother superior was well aware was way beyond the means of Bluebell's guardian, amounting to more than three weeks' wages. So, when she had reached the age of twelve, it was felt that it would be more suitable for her to complete her education at a local Catholic church school, St Paul's, which was a co-educational day school, and where, given the presence of some tough boys, it would be prudent for her to behave herself.

Nearby was the West Derby Golf Course, its commodious clubhouse adjoining the picturesquely-named Yew Tree Lane. Its membership, then as now, was drawn from the middle-class shopkeepers and businessmen of the area, who belonged as much for the convivial social life connected with it as for the exercise involved in whacking the ball around the flat nine-hole course (which has since been doubled) laid out between the trees flanking the placid Deys Brook. There was money to be earned from caddying, and Bluebell, taking her example from some of the boys at her school, decided that she could finance her dancing classes by lugging heavy sets of clubs around the course for the players in their tweed plus-fours and golf-knits. On the strength of her ebullient personality and rosy-cheeked prettiness she

Bluebell as a Madame Cummings fairy

Tiller Girls in the Twenties

became the most popular of the caddies, largely because the players were amused and intrigued by the idea of a young, blue-eyed blonde accompanying them through their game. Some even, in an excess of gallantry, would take pity at her slender frame, and carry the golf-bag themselves, thus defeating the object of hiring a caddy, yet would still part with the customary tip in full at the conclusion of their play. The members would pass on their old irons to the caddies, giving them opportunities to practise strokes for themselves. When the weather was fine, rather than wait for customers inside the caddies' hut they would be outside swinging the clubs, and Bluebell learned to become a proficient golfer.

Another source of much-needed revenue was the paper round. A newsagent's shop served both her district and the one adjoining, which was some notches up on the social scale. By delivering copies of the *Daily Telegraph* and *The Times* each day to houses with proper front gardens, gates and driveways she was able to examine the reading matter of the middle classes, and gain a glimmering of the mysterious processes of British journalism. Today, living in Paris, she keeps her eye on Britain through the *Daily Mail*, a habit formed when it actually published a special daily continental edition, and from numerous Sunday newspapers.

The *Daily Mail* was involved in an early incident in the furtherance of her career. One day, as she was returning from dancing class, she noticed that Shillington's, the newsagents on the corner by the West Derby tram terminus, had a contents bill for that newspaper outside the shop announcing that featured in that day's edition was a 'WEST DERBY BEAUTY'. When she got home she said: 'Auntie Mary! There's a West Derby beauty in the *Mail*. Who could it be?' The answer came as a surprise. 'It's you! I sent your photograph in, and they've printed it.' The newspaper had been running a competition for pretty faces, and had selected that of Bluebell from many hundreds of photographs that had been submitted. There followed shortly afterwards an invitation to go to London to take part in the finals of the contest, but there was no money to spend in Mary Murphy's household for such a speculative venture. In compensation for the missed trip the newspaper sent a postal order for the magnificent sum of half-a-guinea, or ten shillings and sixpence. 'After that the cheeky kids in the street used to call me ten-and-sixpenny face!' recalled Bluebell.

Mary Murphy had seen to it that Bluebell, born a Catholic, was raised within the faith, and expected her charge to attend Mass, even though she herself was working at the hospital on Sundays. On one occasion Bluebell was called back by the priest after the service, and given three rosaries to say for not being at Mass the preceding Sunday. Mary asked her why she had been late coming out of the church. Bluebell answered that the ways of God were indeed mysterious because the Father had been apprised of the knowledge that she had skipped Mass. 'God didn't tell him, I did!' snorted Mary. 'You should have been at Mass, and I'm responsible for you.' Thus was a young faith given an early shaking.

It was difficult for Bluebell to play a large part in the work of St Paul's Church. There were barriers then for single parents, especially those who had no right whatsoever to wear a wedding band. And there were also social distinctions between the prosperous part of the congregation and those who came from the poorer areas in the parish. But Mary Murphy retained her pride and kept the attentions of charities at bay.

When the other children at Bluebell's school went for their summer holidays for a fortnight on the sands of Morecambe or Rhyl, Bluebell had to be content with an afternoon's excursion to the almost local seaside town of New Brighton, reached after a tram journey into Liverpool and a thrilling, blustery voyage on the ferry across the Mersey, with exciting views of the big ships loading and unloading along the dockfront. They would take tea in a flask and a thick pile of sandwiches bound in a teacloth, which as soon as they were unwrapped would become gritty with sand as the wind flew across the flat beach. Nevertheless it was a great treat for the child, who could not even venture as far as Southport, the most popular of Liverpool's nearby seaside towns, because it involved a train journey, and was consequently way beyond their means.

However, the rural character of West Derby in that time in the Twenties offered holiday opportunities on farms to earn small amounts of money. There was the potato picking, for example, a back-stretching task that necessitated an early start at six in the morning, but which Bluebell enjoyed because she could usually inveigle one of the boys to do the heaviest work. She also undertook to deliver milk to the neighbourhood, carrying it in a churn on a large tradesmen's bicycle which had an iron rack over the front wheel. She would ladle the milk into the receptacles proffered at the various

Dancers of the Bal du Moulin Rouge

households on her round. It was before the age of the milk bottle and the processes milk must go through nowadays before it can be sold, and often the rich, creamy liquid was still warm from the cow, milked only an hour or two earlier.

The earnings were placed in a lacquered tin moneybox, and went towards keeping up the dancing classes. Mary Murphy made the dresses, and the little shoes were darned until hardly anything of the original fabric remained. Bluebell had photographs of herself taken in her dancing outfit; the prints cost three for sixpence-halfpenny. It was a good investment; they helped to secure her first professional job, in the children's dancing troupe of a small pantomime when she was twelve. It was staged far away from Liverpool, at Newquay in Cornwall, on the south-western tip of England. The pantomime was *Babes in the Wood*, and it ran for three weeks in a tiny theatre in the wintry seaside resort. Madame Cummings had obtained the engagement for her six most promising pupils, who were given billing as The Six Little Darlings.

Although the youngest in the company, Bluebell had by now grown

The aspirant Bluebell

considerably from the tiny creature she had been as a small child, and was the tallest of the girls, the only one to be challenged by the ticket inspector on the train, suspicious that she was too old to qualify for the juvenile fare. But it was at Newquay that Bluebell realized that her ambition lay in performing on stage before appreciative audiences. Of the modest five shillings she received each week for her efforts she sent half back to Mary Murphy, from whom she was parted for the first time since she had been adopted.

At last childhood was coming to an end for Bluebell. The trip to Newquay during that Christmas holiday had given her the first glimpse of an outside world, since the infant memories of Dublin were too intangible to grasp, and had made her thirsty for travel. She formulated some private resolutions. Yes, she would see the world. And she would have dinner at the Adelphi, Liverpool's largest, grandest, most opulent hotel, where it was customary for the winners of the Grand National to celebrate their triumph at Aintree.

There were other stage shows for the girls of Madame Cummings' classes, and Bluebell excelled. The year after *Babes in the Wood* she appeared in another pantomime, *Sinbad the Sailor*, nearer home, at the Rotunda in Scotland Road, Liverpool. An excited Mary Murphy attended one of the performances and sat in the front row, spending more time scanning the line of young dancers looking for Bluebell than paying attention to the show itself.

When Bluebell turned fourteen the end of her schooling loomed. It was normal then for children to quit full-time education at that age — only those who had been fortunate enough to pass the entrance examination for a grammar school went any further, and their parents, unless the child was exceptional and able to win a scholarship, would be expected to pay fees. Consequently, such places were for the middle classes rather than the poor. It was only the wealthier parents who could afford to send their children to private schools, at which they could stay until they were sixteen or older. The vast majority of children were released from the education system at fourteen, with both employers seeking low-paid help and children aching to escape pedagogic discipline generally considering it not a moment too soon.

It was a sentiment with which Bluebell concurred. The final two years at school had been a bore, and she was impatient to begin her life properly. She was no great shakes as a scholar, but she had a sharp mind, with the ability to grasp essentials very quickly. Her biggest test lay only a little way ahead into her future. She was about to gain some practical experience in one of the few school subjects that excited her — geography.

3   Berlin

BLUEBELL WAS IMPATIENT with school, bored with the narrow life that she was leading, living in the tiny house at 48 Deysbrook Lane, and keen to do something entirely new. Mary Murphy, for all her innumerable foibles such as her fastidiousness over Bluebell's clothes, her strict religiosity and her firm discipline, was very much a pragmatist, and had long realized that the time was rapidly approaching when her young ward would want to be leaving home. Fourteen may seem a relatively young age at which to be contemplating such a step, but in the Twenties most children had by then begun to earn money so that they could at least make a start at supporting themselves.

Bluebell emerged in adolescence as a gangly, loose-limbed blonde with an infectious laugh, quick wits and considerable personal charm. Her direct, open manner was sometimes startling to people for its abruptness, and she gave short shrift to anyone suspected of attempting to get the better of her. The large-eyed, ashen-faced child with weak legs had vanished, replaced by a healthy teenager. The years of toughening up at Madame Cummings' dancing classes had transformed her. Bluebell's vigour and tireless energy are still remarkable, even today when she is in her seventies, and she

31

constantly carries on long after others much younger than herself have succumbed to complete exhaustion. Her robust constitution is the precious legacy passed on to her through the wisdom of Mary Murphy during the years in which she was emerging from childhood, and it is a heritage that she never allows herself to forget.

'Never for a moment do I consider that I had a deprived childhood,' she says. 'Mary Murphy always saw to it that I was well-dressed. And I always had enough jam butties to eat!' In fact, her diet extended considerably beyond mere bread and jam, and while not in the steak-and-oysters bracket, was for the most part both nutritious and healthy. But above everything else, Mary Murphy had allowed her to discover and develop the enthusiasm that was to become not only the overwhelming passion of her life but also a remarkably successful career — dancing.

At the age of fourteen Bluebell was to have another reason for which to thank the extraordinary Irish spinster. A Scottish touring concert party was recruiting young dancers, and Bluebell was accepted for it. It meant leaving home and spending many weeks at a time travelling the length and breadth of Scotland, performing six nights a week. Bluebell said goodbye to her friends at St Paul's School, packed her small brown suitcase and prepared to leave her old home. She remembers how Mary Murphy bought some imitation Astrakhan and sewed it on to the hem of her reefer coat — it was a time in the Twenties when things nautical were much in fashion. The intention was to make Bluebell look older than her fourteen years, and the navy-blue coat with its flashy fur trimmings was meant to give her some measure of sophistication. 'When I wore it,' Bluebell recalls, 'I used to get catcalls from the street youths, and cries like "Does your mother know you're out?" '

Going on the road in a touring show in those days was regarded in some quarters with some disapproval. Had Mary Murphy announced that she intended to hand Bluebell over to the white slave market it is unlikely that she would have met with more hostility from several of her relations, who felt that the kind of life on offer was scarcely suitable for a fourteen-year-old girl. In truth, the troupe, which was known as the Hot Jocks, was really rather respectable. Its repertoire mainly consisted of old ballads sung in a convivial atmosphere, with Neil Nelson, a comedian, telling jokes in a broad Scottish vein. The principals would sit around a table, pretending to quaff ale while singing and joking. The manager of the Hot Jocks, Dave Westwood, also appeared with them, and their principal Scottish dancer was George Clarkson. The six young girl dancers with whom Bluebell was to team, wore, as Clarkson, now in his nineties, recalls, organdie blouses and blue bloomers. It was their job to pound away at lively tap dance routines in between the other turns, and they were a welcome break for both the audience and the rest of the company.

They travelled throughout Scotland, performing in the numerous music

Her first experience of life on the road—Bluebell (second from left) with the Hot Jocks

halls which were still the most popular form of mass entertainment in the Twenties, in spite of the encroachments of the silent cinema, but which have now all disappeared — the Theatre Royal in Dumfries, the Pavilion at Ayr, the Beach Pavilion, Burntisland, the Oddfellows Music Hall in Glasgow, and many others. They would also put the show on in church halls, village halls, assembly rooms — anywhere that was big enough to offer a stage. Occasional forays were made south of the border. Bluebell still shudders with dreadful recollection of the dirty and squalid dressing rooms that were provided in the Lancashire town of Wigan, years before George Orwell was to write a book about the awfulness of the place between the wars.

It was a hectic life for a young teenager, constantly on the move, barely settling down into theatrical digs in strange towns before having to move on to the next engagement. The show invariably finished its run wherever it was on the Saturday night, leaving Sunday free for travelling onwards. Sunday trains in the strictly sabbatarian Scotland of the Twenties were almost the exclusive preserve of the entertainers moving on to their next port-of-call, and a carefree bonhomie might prevail as one group encountered another awaiting their connection on some windswept station platform.

The silent cinema was on its last legs — already in the United States Al Jolson had stupefied audiences and shattered the studio bosses as a result of the Warner Brothers' bold gamble of starring him in *The Jazz Singer*, the first film to exploit properly their new sound-on-disc device, the Vitaphone. Many of the variety houses, including the celebrated Glasgow Coliseum, a 3000-seat theatre owned by Moss Empires, ended live entertainment and became cinemas that were wired-up for talking pictures, thus setting in train the slow decline that would end in the total extinction of the music hall by the Sixties. Glasgow, which once had a score of variety theatres, now has none. The famous Alhambra has been turned into an office block, and the Theatre Royal was for many years the principal studio building for Scottish Television, although more recently it has been returned to live theatre.

Bluebell found the new life she was leading, in spite of the occasional hardships, tremendously exhilarating. The girls shared rooms in their lodgings, and developed the spirit of camaraderie that sometimes mystifies people outside show business. Bluebell proved to be a popular member of the team, always ready with a quick quip to defuse tense situations, and dependably supportive should any of the others be having troubles. Her colleagues were even prepared to forgive her insatiable appetite for hard work, and the drive and energy which she put into her performances. For Bluebell, her period with the Hot Jocks was a very happy time, marking the transition from dependent childhood to grown-up independence. Not that she had much money to make the most of her newly liberated state. From her modest weekly wage of £1 she was sending half, ten shillings, home to Mary Murphy as a debt of honour. (She was to continue supporting her until her death in 1948, with only the war years, when she was behind enemy lines, breaking the flow of cash.) And at the first opportunity on her return to Liverpool for a holiday breather, after the hectic traipsing around Scotland, she fulfilled her own private pledge to herself of having dinner at the Adelphi, and took Mary Murphy as her guest.

The period with the Hot Jocks lasted for around nine months. The end came about quite unexpectedly. It was during her brief sojourn in Liverpool that a friend who, like Bluebell, had been a pupil of Madame Cummings, told her that she had won an important audition, and would welcome some moral support. Bluebell readily agreed to accompany the nervous girl, whose name was Effie, to the rehearsal hall where it was taking place. The seeker of new talent turned out to be a figure of some prominence in the dance world — none other than Alfred Jackson, who ran a team of precision dancers in various European venues, but mostly in Germany, where he was based. Effie duly went through her paces, satisfactorily as it turned out, and then the great man himself asked her when her friend was also going to dance. Bluebell said that she had come only to support Effie, and had no intention of auditioning since she already had a job. Jackson, who was unused to girls turning down the opportunity of auditioning for him, was intrigued, and urged her to have a go anyway, if only for future reference, as no jobs lasted for ever. The problem of a lack of dancing attire was

Bluebell (second from the right) and the Hot Jocks, touring in Scotland

overcome by Effie, who offered to lend Bluebell her leotard and shoes, and so finally the audition took place.

Alfred Jackson was impressed by Bluebell's performance. 'I'd like to talk to your mother,' he said when she had finished her steps. 'You can see my Auntie!' said Bluebell. Mary Murphy was then duly invited to meet him at the Adelphi, where he was staying while he was in Liverpool. He told her that Bluebell was just the sort of dancer that he needed for his company, and that were she to join him she would be very well looked after. He was offering to pay her £2 a week, and she would be able to live quite easily on only ten shillings, or a quarter of her wages, as board and lodging would be provided. Bluebell therefore would be in a position to send home thirty shillings a week, an amount which to Mary Murphy seemed like unparalleled riches. Moreover, she would be assured that Bluebell was in the best of hands. Even if Alfred Jackson's girls should find themselves dancing in the more notorious European centres of unbridled behaviour the stern chaperonage of Jackson's forbidding German-born wife, Frau Ellie, ensured that no harm befell them. Had Bluebell been entering a convent as a novitiate she could scarcely expect to have a more protected existence, according to Jackson.

He was a respected figure in the world of theatrical entertainment. Originally he had been part of the same music hall act, The Eight Lancashire Lads, a team of clog dancers well known before the First World War, in which Charlie Chaplin had begun his career. From there he had progressed to becoming one of the leading managers of dance companies in Europe, and he also had a permanent troupe under contract to the Folies

35

Alfred Jackson, second from right, with the Eight Lancashire Lads

Bergère. With all his outlets it was scarcely surprising that places among the Jackson Girls were greatly sought after.

Bluebell returned to Scotland to continue working with the Hot Jocks, refusing to be seduced by new offers. But after a few days she received a letter from Mary Murphy instructing her to hand in her notice and return to Liverpool as soon as possible, because, whether she liked it or not, she was going to be a Jackson Girl, and would be going off to Germany. Dave Westwood, the manager of the Hot Jocks, was greatly distressed when Bluebell told him what was happening, and immediately offered her another ten shillings a week, if it would help to persuade her Auntie Mary to allow her to stay on in his company. Bluebell, who had become principal dancer, was intensely loyal even though the show was of little consequence, and still retained a touching childhood innocence. She was perfectly willing to remain with them on these new, improved terms, but Mary Murphy was having none of it. 'In those days you did what you were told!' recalled Bluebell. Which meant that she would have to take the plunge and become a Jackson Girl on the continent of Europe.

Her departure from the Hot Jocks was an occasion of sadness and high emotion. She had become very fond of the little company of no more than a dozen itinerant performers, and knew that, whatever happened to her, she

Alfred Jackson with some of his Girls en route for a Twenties Canadian tour

would always miss the remarkable friendliness that prevailed within the group. She had never left the British Isles before, and now she was setting out for a strange foreign country. Mary Murphy arranged the acquisition of a passport, and booked her passage, which involved a lengthy cross-country rail journey to the port of Harwich, and then a North Sea crossing which would take her to the Hook of Holland, where she would have to catch a train that would travel all the way to Berlin. There were two other girls making the same journey, one of them her friend Effie who had been at the audition. All three of them were neophytes as far as travelling abroad was concerned. In the Twenties only a fraction of the numbers of Britons who travel today to Europe made journeys abroad, and in the days before mass air transit it was an arduous and lengthy adventure. The bustle on the quayside at the Hook after the steamer had berthed following its voyage from England was a fascinating sight to a girl raised in one of Europe's principal seaports. Awaiting the girls after they had cleared customs was a huge train, the longest Bluebell had ever seen, with white metal plates slung below the windows at the end of the carriages listing a string of unpronounceable destinations she had never heard of, but concluding in bolder type than the rest with 'BERLIN'. Shortly after they had found their third-class seats it started on its way, and Bluebell fell asleep, jerking awake a few minutes later as the train heaved itself into the big central station at Rotterdam. She woke again as they reached the German border shortly after Hengelo, and produced her clean, almost unstamped passport in its stiff navy-blue cover for the German immigration official who boarded the train. After that the train trundled through the dark night across the sleeping North German plain until it eventually came to the big capital of the Fatherland, Berlin.

Although Berlin was one of Europe's principal cities, the seat of the government at that time was at Weimar, where it had been established following the humiliating Versailles peace treaty of 1919. Bluebell arrived in Germany at the tail end of an era known as '*Die Goldenen Zwanziger Jahre*' (The Golden Twenties), when the city's reputation for thrill-seeking and diversionary entertainment rivalled and, in a number of ways, eclipsed that of Paris. There was a vast range of performing arts on offer, ranging from tiny basement cabarets where avant-garde poetry, outspoken political satire and transvestism could provide the basis for revues, to the other extreme, the gigantic Grosse Schauspielhaus, where an audience of nearly 5000 people could gawp at a spectacular stage performance employing a huge cast and elaborate special effects. There was no censorship and little restraint. Berlin nightlife was haunted by homosexuals and lesbians, fetishists and transvestites. It was the period described so vividly by Christopher Isherwood, and later glamorized out of recognition in the Broadway musical *Cabaret*. But by 1927 there were already plenty of Nazi agitators stirring up trouble, going for the soft and flabby underbelly of the hedonistic city. The Jewish population was already suffering from their attacks, which, as the movement became more organized, grew ever more violent. It was 1927, and Adolf Hitler's tract on Nazism, *Mein Kampf*, had recently been published, and only another six years would pass before he would be in full power and poised to create the Third Reich, which would stifle the spirit of liberalism and unbridled free comment that had prevailed before.

Bluebell hated Berlin on sight. Not only was it larger, noisier and uglier than she had expected, but she felt a deep sense of alienation through her inability to communicate in German. She had made the transition from a humble touring concert party working in mainly small country towns in Scotland to one of the leading dancing troupes in the world, working in a gigantic theatre in an unfamiliar continental city. The big fish from the little pond was now a mackerel in the North Sea. She found that as the new girl in a large troupe she was going to get the blame for mistakes — that was the way it worked. She was now part of an organized, if not regimented, corps of chorus girls. There were thirty of them in line on the stage. Their lives were carefully overseen. They all lived in a typical tall Berlin *pension*, a narrow multi-storeyed building a few streets from the theatre. Four girls were assigned to each room, two to a bed. The problems of thirty young women sharing only two bathrooms between them were too horrific to contemplate, particularly as the time drew near for them to go to the theatre. Even that was accomplished in a highly disciplined, almost ritualistic manner. They formed up to make a crocodile line in pairs, rather like convent schoolgirls. There was a double purpose — not only did it protect them from the attentions of an eager male populace and ensure that all the girls remained together, but Alfred Jackson also appreciated the advertising value, since the onlookers in the sidewalk cafés would be more than mildly curious to know who these astonishing beauties parading past in line were, and would take the trouble to find out.

The Scala Theatre in the Lutherstrasse was enormous, larger than any Bluebell had seen before. The stage was wide enough to accommodate the line of thirty Jackson Girls, and their precision dance routines were regarded as one of the sights of Berlin. They appeared several times during the show, between other acts in a variety revue. When the curtain came down, and they had exchanged their costumes for their street clothes, they would go back to the boarding house, closely watched by the hawk-like Frau Ellie, Alfred Jackson's wife. She was, as Bluebell recalls, a typical German *hausfrau*.

Bluebell in Berlin (right) and on first visit to Paris (above)

'She was a very heavy lady. When we went out to buy dresses at various chain stores she would gasp at the flimsy things we found. She'd say "I go round the shops and I never see dresses like that!" She always had a permanent wave, and like most stout people she perspired heavily. I used to feel quite sorry for her.'

Alfred Jackson also had a mistress, Tessie, a German girl who was the captain of his Berlin troupe. Although the relationship was handled with reasonable discretion Frau Ellie could scarcely have been unaware of it. However, in public at any rate she chose to ignore it.

As far as the other girls were concerned, there were, for all the constant chaperoning, occasional opportunities to stir the passions, albeit in ways that nowadays appear to be innocent, if not naïve. Bluebell recalls being entranced by a Danish tenor, Max Hansen, who was in the show, because his act followed one of the appearances of the Jackson Girls, and each night he would come on stage from the same side on which they made their exit, and always grasp the last girl on the line — who happened to be Bluebell.

More ambitiously, she found a way of escaping from the prison-like lodgings, but the method required considerable co-operation from the other girls, and astonishing nerve. She met a dancer called Rudolph Grunig, who was appearing in the ballet at the Berlin State Opera and who was much interested in her. He invited her to a midnight gala ball which was being held for the opera house. Bluebell resolved to go, come what may, and on the night in question after she returned from the Scala with the other girls she surreptitiously hid her handbag under a bush outside the building. Later, she threw her shoes out of the window of her bedroom some forty feet from the ground, and then she coolly eased herself out on to the window ledge and grabbed an adjacent drainpipe. She was wearing a dress with a frilled hem, and so tied some elastic around her waist, tucking the garment carefully around it, leaving her legs clear so that her descent would not be impeded by a flapping skirt. Luckily there was no one around at that hour to observe the dangerous and indecorous spectacle, and she reached the street safely to go off to her illicit, glamorous night out, with her scarlet party dress still reasonably intact. The return at five-thirty in the morning proved, however, to be more difficult. Getting down the drainpipe was easy compared with getting up it. She was dependent on the other girls, who had been watching out for her. Her escort had discreetly stopped his car at the end of the street, and the lookout girl at the window spotted Bluebell approaching on foot. The window was opened and in the best Angela Brazil schoolgirl tradition a rope of knotted-together sheets was lowered, which Bluebell proceeded to climb, hand-over-hand, having again used the conveniently placed bush to hide her shoes and handbag. The three girls in the bedroom held on tightly to the sheets — had their grip faltered Bluebell's long career might well have been thwarted on that night.

'I was lucky to get away with it,' said Bluebell, recalling the incident. 'If

The Jackson Girls at the Folies Bergère

the sheets had been torn I would have been in trouble with the landlady. And if I had been found out I would have been sent home immediately — they were very strict in those days. And as for my gorgeous red dress — I'm afraid that it was absolutely filthy.'

As soon as the front door of the *pension* was opened up at 7.30 Bluebell raced down and retrieved her possessions from under the bush, making sure that no one saw her. It had been a totally sleepless night, not just for her but for her room-mates, who had not had the excitement of the perilous climb and the pleasure of a night out, away from the fierce scrutiny of Frau Ellie. 'When you are that age you can survive these things, you know, simply because they are so exciting,' said Bluebell.

In any case, the day for the Jackson Girls was a long one. Each morning at ten there was a dance class, finishing at noon. The rhythm would be set by the clashing of a tambourine, and the girls in a precision line would do their high kicks to its insistent beat. It was exhausting work. Afterwards it would be time to return to the lodgings for lunch, which always had to be attended. The afternoons were free for shopping or resting, and for taking tea with the other girls. It was this period which Bluebell had used for her covert meetings with her ballet friend, usually for aperitifs at Kranzler's, where the Friedrichstrasse met the Unter den Linden, the Berliner equivalent of the Champs-Elysées. At five-thirty the girls were required to be back at the *pension* for their evening meal, again a compulsory occasion, and after it they would march off to the theatre in their two-by-two formation, with their confident captain, Tessie, at the front setting the pace. Alfred Jackson ensured that everyone was together, and that no stragglers were lost. His girls were forbidden to socialize with any of the employees of the theatre, or members of the orchestra and other acts. Any transgressions could result in instant dismissal. Thus his girls were rendered mysterious, unattainable and tantalizing, in strange contrast with the outrageously permissive atmosphere prevailing in Berlin in the last years before the Nazis came into power. Even their days off were often devoted to publicity sessions, and the girls were photographed boating together and frolicking in a somewhat artificial manner in the city parks, or sightseeing at the chief tourist landmarks. It was a very regimented company.

'We accepted all this,' said Bluebell, 'because that was the way we heard it was going to be. Of course, it would be totally ridiculous and unacceptable to treat girls like that nowadays, and even when I started my own group in the Thirties it wasn't like that. But you have to remember that this was very many years ago.'

4   **The Folies**

THE STRICT REGIME under which the Jackson Girls were expected to live was enforced as strongly on tour as it was when they were playing at their home base in Berlin. They appeared at the Scala for about five months in the year, but sixteen of the thirty girls in the company would spend much of the rest of the time travelling to other German cities. They would always play at the leading theatres, such as the Hansa, Hamburg. There was a group of prestige houses in Leipzig, Dusseldorf, Cologne and Munich which were invariably on the Jackson circuit during their break from the Scala. The girls would travel in third-class railway carriages, with wooden seats, eight to each compartment. On long journeys they would push their luggage out into the corridor. Then two girls would sleep on the net luggage racks over the seats, with the rest using the seats and floor to lie full-length in cramped, uncomfortable slumber. They were not even permitted to go to the dining car, but were expected to subsist on their specially prepared sandwiches, washed down with milky coffee from Thermos flasks.

Bluebell by now had already had a brief romantic interlude in her life — in Liverpool. It had developed through her friendship with a girl called Todd Smith, whose parents were caretakers at a big residence in the Leyfield

Road, close to the convent where Bluebell had gone to school. The Smiths lived in the lodge, and Bluebell was sometimes a teatime visitor there. Todd had an older brother, Sam, who was the chauffeur at the house, and he and Bluebell eventually became very good friends. Their chumminess annoyed one of Mary Murphy's relations, who argued that as Sam was a Protestant the affair should go no further. Sam was an engineer by calling, but had failed to find a job in the depressed economic climate of Britain. He had no intention, however, of remaining a chauffeur. Since opportunities at home were so scarce he decided to emigrate to Australia.

'He wanted me to marry him, and go out there,' said Bluebell. 'I told him that he would have to go first, and find a job. He could then send for me. Well, that's just what he did. Except that by then I had gone to Germany, and I had to write to him and say that I much preferred my new life to the one he was offering. He later married an Australian girl, had two children, and lived the rest of his life very happily in Perth.'

In 1985 he was reported to be in retirement, having spent his career as an officer in the Western Australian Fire Brigade.

After a few months at the Scala, Bluebell found herself assigned to a team of Jackson Girls who would travel outside Germany. Initially they went to Copenhagen, then to Spain and Hungary, making the long journey from Barcelona to Budapest in one horrific third-class train ride. Bluebell had two long stays in Hungary, the first engagement lasting for three months, the second for two.

There was also a brief period in London, in variety at the London Coliseum, the famous theatre in St Martin's Lane, within sight of Trafalgar Square. Top of the bill while the Jacksons were playing there was the American 'hot' singer, Sophie Tucker, who took a shine to Bluebell.

'I was a wide-eyed child, and I used to like standing in the wings to watch this wonderful star. She had her own band on the stage, and I had never seen anyone like her — the way she used to belt out those great songs of hers. After a week or so she said "You like watching me, kid? Come back and talk to me in my dressing room!" I remember her telling me, "If you want to make it, you've got to work hard, honey!" She was a very great lady, who radiated energy, and she had a heart of gold.'

The season at the Coliseum lasted for four weeks. The sixteen girls who had come over from Germany performed four different numbers at various points in the evening, in between the other acts. The notorious crocodile line, familiar on the continent, did not apply in London because their theatrical digs were four miles away from the theatre, in the South London district of Brixton, which in those days was much favoured by light entertainers for reasonably priced accommodation. The girls made the journey to and from Brixton and the theatre on a regular red 'General' double-decker bus, with an outside staircase spiralling down its stern.

Immediately after the last show on Saturday nights Bluebell would race

Les Sirenes de Ceylan: a Jackson Folies Bergère number

from the theatre to Euston station, arriving just in time to catch the last train to Liverpool, to which it would be bearing the following day's Sunday newspapers, and a few late-returning football supporters. The long, steam-hauled journey took five hours of sitting bolt upright on a hard third-class seat, but would get her home with enough time to spend a few hours there before rushing back to Lime Street station and the last train of the evening to the south, getting to Brixton in sufficient time for the rehearsal call first thing on Monday morning. It was an exhausting way to spend a weekend, but Bluebell felt that it was well worth it.

A nostalgic recreation of the Folies promenoir from the Fiftieth anniversary show

The brief glimpse she had received of West End life turned out to be a pleasant foretaste of her next exciting experience. In the summer of 1930 she was asked to go to Paris as a holiday replacement for the girls at the Folies Bergère. She fell completely under the spell of the magic spectacle she found at the world-famous theatre in the Rue Richer. Never before had she seen such imaginative sets, dazzling lighting displays or decorative costumes. It was the period when designers of the calibre of Erté were producing breath-taking creations. There were also the justly celebrated nudes, who for the most part consisted of statuesque girls whose sculpted breasts were proudly displayed, but never the crutch area which was always discreetly, and sometimes tantalizingly, masked. Given such glamour it was scarcely surprising that Sam Smith was doomed not to win Bluebell — she had found a far more enticing alternative on the stage, in theatrical spectacle.

The Folies Bergère had first opened in 1869, twenty years before another world-famous centre of Paris nightlife, the Moulin Rouge. Its earliest days were somewhat marred by the Franco-Prussian war of 1870 and the siege of Paris, which put an immediate stop to frivolous light entertainment, and for a brief period the hall was a political rallying point, as the Commune made its brief, abruptly curtailed appearance on the French national stage.

After the bloodshed and deprivations undergone by the population during that unhappy era the Folies was able to revert to its originally intended purpose, and became renowned for the personable qualities of its *corps de ballet*. It also gathered notoriety for its *promenoir*, the wide, open area at the rear of the auditorium, which was ostensibly to permit patrons to wander in from the bar and casually observe the events on the stage without the tiresome bother of having to make their way to their seats. It was not long before it became one of the principal picking-up points for some of the gaudiest prostitutes in Paris, and the acts on the stage were often required to compete with what to modern sensibilities would have seemed like a noisy cocktail party going on at the back of the theatre. The old Empire Theatre in Leicester Square, London had been designed on similar lines, and such activities were to be found there, too, which excited the blue-noses of the day when they had nothing better to denounce.

The nudes came much later to the Folies Bergère. Striptease is said to have started in Paris in the 1890s, but not at the Folies. It probably originated in the smaller music halls of Montmartre. *Tableaux vivants*, in which stiffly posed performers re-enacted famous paintings, often those hanging in the Louvre, gave such spectacles a spurious cultural cachet, and there was usually plenty of simulated nudity. These shows were common in most European capitals. The skin-toned body stockings of the period, long before the invention of stretchy, figure-hugging man-made fibres, usually revealed unsightly wrinkles. In Britain, under the strict rulings of the Lord Chamberlain, whose office since the Restoration had been responsible for licensing theatrical performances, the *tableaux vivants* were the only form of stage nudity permitted until the Sixties, and even the famous nudes at the Windmill Theatre in the Second World War were not permitted to twitch a muscle without incurring legal wrath. Such 'peek-a-boo' strippers as Phyllis Dixey frequently found themselves in trouble when their feathered fans accidentally slipped during a performance.

It is a matter of historical record that the first exposed female breast was seen on the Folies stage in 1907. Its owner was more famous as one of the greatest French twentieth-century fiction writers, Colette. Her brief career as a music-hall performer following her early divorce is featured in three of her books, including *La Vagabonde*, a novel in which she drew extensively on her theatre experiences.

Below: Mannequin Nu
from Femmes en Folie

*Above: an Erte costume
design for the Folies*

Left: Paul Derval, the brilliant Folies administrator
Overleaf: a typical Derval spectacular

The undraped female form became more and more an element of the shows, in all probability encouraged by saucy French periodicals, of which *La Vie Parisienne* was the undoubted leader. The *poilu* in the First World War had marched to the front with the sound of bugles ringing in his ear, but with the latest issue of the magazine in his rucksack, and when he got to the trenches he would adorn the dug-out walls with the exquisitely-drawn plates within its pages by Raphaël Kirchner, the inventor of the pin-up girl. Memories of the girls at the Folies and their magnificent breasts somehow became symbolic in the military consciousness of the France that had to be fought for and saved. In other words, by then the Folies Bergère was already enshrined as a national monument.

When the war was over the catalytic force behind the success of the theatre was Paul Derval, who had earlier been a stage comedian, and who had an extravagant taste for colour and spectacle. He became the administrator of the Folies in 1918, and was to remain in charge there until his death in 1966. During his long reign some thirty different productions were staged, and many stars were made by their appearances on the boards there, or had their reputations enhanced by the association. Maurice Chevalier, Mistinguett, Josephine Baker, Yvonne Printemps and Charles Trenet were some of them.

During the Twenties Derval introduced more and more nudity, which, when seen in the context of the sumptuous costumes and sets, became the trademark of the Folies Bergère. Paradoxically, the act was being cleaned up, and, whatever passions were excited by the displays of female flesh on the stage, the notorious *promenoir* lost its prostitutes, not suddenly, but by gradual and increasingly firm vigilance on the part of the management. And to further entrench the respectability of his theatre, Derval sent touring companies out to the more strait-laced cities in other countries, with sets of

tinsel stars in varying sizes in the wardrobe trunks, their powers of concealment graded to whatever local notions of permissiveness would deem acceptable in each destination. Needless to say, a complete cover-up was necessary in the United Kingdom since only totally immobile nude figures were permitted, and movement was the essence of Derval's shows.

There was a distinction between the dancers and the showgirls, the latter merely having to move gracefully and display costumes, and their group was further sub-divided into the *mannequins nues* and the *mannequins habillées*. Derval was at pains to assure the world that they were all nice girls, and their morals were carefully checked. Even casual flirtations within the theatre were ruthlessly suppressed, and the Alfred Jackson Girls were marched nightly to and from the theatre as a crocodile team, just as in Berlin, thus thwarting the hopeful stage-door Johnnies who gathered in the Rue Saulnier after performances in the hope of singling out their special favourites. Unlike many other Parisian music halls the Folies regarded the girls as a main attraction in their own right, and not subordinate to the headlining stars, and so they enjoyed a special mystique. If male patrons sent notes backstage the captain's job was to tear them up, and share out gifts if there was insufficient information to show where they could be returned.

Bluebell realized that in her line of business there could be no greater goal than to be part of the Folies Bergère company — there was nowhere else in the world capable of presenting so many opportunities to an ambitious stage dancer.

After her first taste of life at the Folies she had returned to Germany. She was now eighteen, and becoming eager to move on from being one of the Scala chorus. In the following summer, 1931, she again went to Paris as a holiday replacement. This time she decided that she would make an attempt to stay there and, if that proved impossible, to quit Alfred Jackson. It transpired that the captain of the girl dancers had, in spite of discouragements, become engaged and wished to leave the Folies in order to get married. Captains were exempted by Jackson from the strict rules he applied to the rest of the girls, largely for his personal convenience in order that he could pursue his relationship with Tessie in Berlin. In this instance he was placed on the spot by his laxity. But Bluebell had the good fortune to make her pitch at just the right moment, when he suddenly needed a good dancer in Paris. Bluebell was offered the job, which she gratefully accepted, and immediately began to think of making Paris her home.

There was, however, to be a setback. Europe, following in the wake of the United States, faced a serious financial crisis in 1931, with companies collapsing in bankruptcy, unemployment spiralling into many millions and private fortunes being wiped out overnight as shares plunged into worthlessness. The dismal economy had an inevitable effect on Paris nightlife, and the Folies, in common with scores of lesser establishments,

The saucy periodical,
La Vie Parisienne,
—reading matter for les poilus

found that its takings were dwindling steeply through the absence of patrons with spending power, yet on the other hand production costs and all the overheads associated with the lavishly mounted shows were not diminishing. Derval gathered everyone on the stage, not merely the performers, but the administrative staff, the stagehands, and even his fellow members of the board of directors, and he asked them in view of the grave situation the theatre was facing to take a ten per cent cut in their earnings. Alfred Jackson, in a state of shock, found the proposal totally unacceptable. On the following day he went to see Derval privately in his office, and argued that, in spite of everything else that was wrong, his dancers could not be faulted, and indeed were the principal attraction of the place. Derval, however, was not to be swayed. For the sake of fairness the cuts must be applied across the board, and affect everybody. Jackson, glum and distressed, called the girls together on stage and told them they were on a month's notice. He had attempted to outbluff Derval and had only succeeded in pushing himself into a corner from which he felt he could not emerge without loss of authority and prestige, and thus could only resign.

53

It was scarcely the best of times to be out of work. Although people in the theatre accept such setbacks as a normal occupational hazard and cheerfully set off to seek another job, it was impossible as far as Bluebell was concerned to contain her despair at seeing a plum position slide away. Jackson had promised to try to find some places in Germany, but the axes were falling there as well, and all he could do after dismissing the bulk of the girls was to invite Bluebell and a German girl called Elfie back to pave the way for reforming the Alfred Jackson Girls as soon as the economy improved. Bluebell once again found herself on the train to Germany, and was promised her wages in full so that she could continue to support Mary Murphy. When she arrived it became apparent that Jackson, shattered by the collapse of his business, did not want to pick up the threads right away. Instead, he proposed that the two girls should accompany his wife and himself first to their home at Frankfurt-on-Main, and then for a short holiday in Bavaria. During the warm summer days they travelled and amused themselves, temporarily putting aside the trauma of recent weeks. Although in contrast it was a placid experience, there was one moment of some excitement. The girls had taken themselves out on to the Main for a river excursion in a tiny boat operated by hand-turned paddles. With startling rapidity what had been a calm summer afternoon suddenly welled up into a fierce storm, and the formerly smooth river surface erupted into tall, raging waves which threatened to swamp and sink the small craft. The force of the current was too much for the girls, and it was impossible for them to steer it to the shore. It was fortunate that their plight had not gone unobserved, and a larger boat was able to reach them to pull the soaked, frightened girls into the river bank, where they scrambled ashore hastily. Thunder and lightning, coupled with a torrential downpour, had wrecked their summer peace.

The short holiday lengthened to six weeks, and Bluebell became impatient with prolonged inactivity, even though she was still being paid for doing nothing. She suspected that Jackson, suffering from the shock of rejection by the Folies Bergère, had lost his will and, in his dejected state, was incapable of getting things together again. The dancers had all been dispersed and no attempts had been made to draw them back together. Eventually he was forced to admit that he felt that he was too old to start afresh, and would prefer a quiet retirement. Bluebell realized that the time had come for her to part company with him, and accordingly she broke the news, having made plans to return to England to look for work there.

Some of the girls who had been with Jackson in Paris had found jobs at the newly opened Leicester Square Theatre, and that became the first place on Bluebell's list when she reached London. The smart West End cinema had been built by the hyper-talented star, Jack Buchanan, an all-round entertainer who was a singer, dancer, actor and light comedian and one of the most successful show-business figures in pre-war Britain. He had

Bluebell leading her dancers at the Folies

intended his new building to be a live theatre, which he would manage, but he and his partner had made a miscalculation and failed to acquire property behind the site, so there was inadequate space for a full-sized stage. In consequence, it became a cinema, with variety performances laid on between the first-run films. Buchanan had a luxuriously furnished flat near the roof of the building, which he continued to use until a German bomb destroyed it in October 1940, but he had long before relinquished any control over the policy of the theatre, which passed to a succession of film companies.

The girls who danced there in cine-variety at the beginning of the Thirties were in a troupe run by Alfred Jackson's brother, John William, who was known as 'J.W.' He walked in while she was talking to her former colleagues from the Folies Bergère, and asked, with some astonishment, what she was doing there, since he thought that she was with his brother in Germany. Bluebell told him that she had left Alfred Jackson in some

Les Bluebells, with their leader at the rear

frustration, and was on her way to Liverpool that same evening. 'J.W.' immediately recalled that he had in the past several times said to Bluebell, even in his brother's presence, that if she ever left the Alfred Jackson Girls he would be very happy for her to go to work for him. He now decided to be as good as his word, and invited Bluebell upstairs to talk to him in his office. When the door was closed and he was seated at his desk he said to her: 'What would you rather do? Work with me here at the Leicester Square Theatre, or go back to Paris, where I can give you a job at the Casino de Paris?' Without hesitation Bluebell opted for a return to Paris, and shortly afterwards she left the theatre, heading not for Euston and the train to Liverpool but the night ferry platform at Victoria Station. The following morning she was back in Paris, the city which had now become the place in which she wanted to spend her life.

The Casino de Paris, in the Rue de Clichy, had an international renown only a notch or two lower than that of the Folies Bergère, and had featured nudes on its stage long before its more distinguished rival. It was something of a shock, therefore, for Bluebell to find that its standards were by comparison nowhere near as high. The captain found her a girl to rehearse with who was a mediocre dancer, and Bluebell then discovered that the majority of the others were as bad. She considered that the performance on her first night there was so poor that she felt that for the sake of her reputation she could not work with such an incompetent company, and offered her resignation. It was, she said, a waste of all Mary Murphy's hard-earned money spent on dancing lessons to end up in a troupe that worked so badly, and was so indifferent to giving their customers a show that was worth the high ticket prices. The next morning she put a call through to J.W. Jackson in London, letting him know exactly how she felt about it. Somewhat amazed, he asked her to stay on for at least a month, after which time he would make her the captain, but she was adamant, and refused to alter her position. As soon as it was feasible to get a replacement for her sent from London she left.

All the time that this drama was taking place enquiries were being made at the Folies by Paul Derval. He was intrigued to know what Bluebell was doing back in Paris. When he learned that she was unhappy with the Casino de Paris Derval asked his informant if Bluebell could be persuaded to come round to the Folies and see him on the following afternoon at 3 p.m. Bluebell turned up on time, and he told her that he would be pleased to offer a contract enabling her to form her own group of dancers for the new show that he was intending to stage, and was due to go into rehearsal almost immediately. At that time it was the custom for the Folies to open with a new production each autumn. Bluebell was expected to be the captain of a dozen girls whom she would be personally responsible for engaging. There could be no hesitation in agreeing to such an attractive proposition, and Bluebell accepted with alacrity, then returned to the Casino to get ready for the evening performance. Word, however, spread quickly, and a day or two later she had an anguished cable from Alfred Jackson, who had been told the news by his brother in London. Jackson virtually ordered her not to sign with the Folies, looking on such an action as disloyal in view of his own unfortunate situation with regard to Derval. Bluebell replied that it was too late, she had already made the deal, and there was nothing that Jackson could do about it. She had severed her link with him, and although he had been instrumental in getting her mainstream dancing career launched, and had presented her with several superb opportunities for advancement, she realized that it would have been foolishly sentimental to have yielded to such a difficult request. The Jackson years were over, even if the man himself was having difficulty in coming to terms with the hard facts.

Shortly afterwards Jackson faced the inevitable and went into full retirement, moving from Frankfurt to Switzerland. His wife, the long-suffering Frau Ellie, pre-deceased him, magnanimously urging from her deathbed that he should marry Tessie, his German mistress who had been his captain in Berlin and the leading dance demonstrator for his troupe. He did precisely that, and spent the rest of his life with Tessie in an English seaside town on the south coast.

5 Birth of the Bluebells

THE NEW SHOW AT THE FOLIES BERGERE was due to open on 5th November 1932. If a day should be designated as the official birth date of the Bluebell Girls it should be that one, for it was then that the first group bearing her name made its debut. The designation came about through a process of natural emergence during rehearsals. The new group of girls being broken in by Bluebell would have to have a name. Bluebell was both a striking and a pretty name. What then could be simpler? In fact the billing for their first show, *Nuits de Folies*, described the group as 'The Blue Bell's Girls' but no one noticed this Gallic mangling and bisection of the word until the programmes were off the presses.

The girls still lived in the apartment building at 50 Rue de Paradis where the Jackson girls had lodged, but Bluebell relaxed the two-by-two rule, and no longer insisted that the dancers should move in a crocodile line to and from the theatre. Derval maintained strictness about in-house flirtations, however. Life for a girl working at the Folies had to be seen to be above reproach. A natural consequence of the regime was that the presence of the rules made the game that much more exciting, and members of the orchestra in particular were well-placed to catch the girls' eyes.

The pianist at the Folies Bergère was a Rumanian *émigré*, who had come to Paris in the first instance in 1922 at the age of eighteen in order to further his musical studies at the Conservatoire. He had, however, abandoned the classical masters for the glitter and glamour of show business, a route he had gone along after working as a pianist in the cinema, accompanying silent films. It had been necessary for him to work in order to pay for his tuition, but the sustained performing, for hours at a stretch, had blunted his concert technique. Oozing charm, good looks and smooth manners, the dashing young man had entranced several of the girls without becoming entangled in awkward commitments.

The musician's name was Marcel Leibovici. He had first met Bluebell during her first short stint at the Folies with the Jackson Girls, and had been intrigued by her blonde vivacity, as well as by her apparent indifference towards him. Eventually the ice was broken and they became friends, but fell out of touch when the Jackson troupe was disbanded. It was Marcel, however, who alerted Paul Derval to Bluebell's new presence in Paris at the Casino, and in effect engineered her return to the Folies in the enhanced circumstances that would lead to the formation of her very own dance group. Their romance was slow to develop, and underwent various setbacks, for Marcel was intelligent, suave and possessed of a keen eye for attractive girls, a commodity scarcely in short supply at the Folies Bergère, while Bluebell was intensely proud, ambitious, dedicated to her craft and career, and certainly unwilling to play a subordinate role to other females.

In the Thirties Folies shows usually played from the autumn of one year until the autumn of the next, a short period by today's standards, when usually a run of at least five years is necessary, given the gigantic costs involved in mounting a production. *Nuits de Folies* came to an end and was superseded by the new show, *Folies en Folie* (it was a superstitious tradition that each Folies Bergère show had to have a 13-letter title) which went into rehearsal. Its star was to be the legendary Mistinguett, a performer who had years earlier become one of France's national institutions. Erté, whose set and costume designers had enhanced many of her shows at the Folies, said of her: 'She was rather ugly, but had a wonderful presence.' Mistinguett had been on the stage since 1897, and was by now more than sixty years of age, although it scarcely seemed credible, given her *gamine* smile and perfectly-shaped legs, which had given cause for more than one generation of Frenchmen to catch their breaths. In time she became the most famous star of the Paris music hall, renowned for her magnificently stately descents of staircases in tall, ostrich-feathered head-dresses and lengthy trains, her silken-covered legs fully displayed. Said Harold Hobson, the former drama critic of *The Sunday Times* and an ardent Francophile: 'She made known without equivocation the full splendour of the human body, adorned or unadorned.' Her legs were insured for a million pounds at Lloyd's of London, although the premium required is not known. When he

Mistinguett, a legend of the Paris stage

was at an early stage in his career, Maurice Chevalier, although many years her junior, became Mistinguett's partner and lover, and always, not withstanding the acrimonious collapse of their affair, which had lasted for a decade, generously paid tribute to the assistance she had given him in attaining his own considerable fame.

Bluebell found Mistinguett a lofty, unapproachable figure. 'She wasn't the kind of person who would be nice to chorus girls — she had tremendous style, and lots of gay boys around her. You rarely said hello to her. As far as I was concerned I never had any conversation with her, and I was never invited into her dressing room. She was a very hard worker, and expected as much from everyone else. But we really had nothing to do with her — we were just the people behind her when she went on stage. And what a devoted following she had among audiences! Having her in the show at all was for the Folies Bergère a tremendous achievement.'

Bluebell inevitably ran into trouble with the formidable 'Miss'. In the new show there was a number in which the chorus were dressed as frogs, the conclusion of which was a leap through a curtain which had been painted to represent a lake. There were various gaps in it, and mattresses were placed behind to catch the girls as they sailed through. It was a complicated and physically demanding routine, calling not only for acrobatic skills but for very precise timing. Bluebell was anxious to rehearse it thoroughly in order that it should work on stage without any hiccups. There was a rehearsal room beneath the stage and Bluebell took her team down there, to put them through several gruelling run-throughs. Unfortunately, not only Bluebell but everyone else became so absorbed in what they were doing that they failed to hear their music cue indicating it was time for them to make their appearance on the stage. There followed pandemonium and hysteria, exacerbated by the great star's outburst of bad temper. She denounced Bluebell for lack of professionalism and fired her and the girls on the spot. Derval was forced with reluctance to comply with her wishes for the sake of the show's well-being, and the Bluebells found themselves out of the show, and for that matter, out of the Folies Bergère itself.

The replacement group for the Bluebells was the Buddy Bradley Girls. Bradley was American and currently very much in fashion. His team specialized in modern jazz and tap, rather than the precision work favoured by the Bluebells. It has always been Bluebell's suspicion that Mistinguett was already committed to having Buddy Bradley in her show, and had been looking for an opportunity to axe her team. The missed-cue incident had thus played right into her hands.

But from the ashes of disaster there was soon to follow a rapid salvation. Another job immediately became available for Bluebell. The Paramount cinema, on the Boulevard des Capucines, close to the Opéra, was one of the largest and most ornate of the old-style picture palaces in Paris, and its director, René Lebreton, echoing the policy of the Radio City Music Hall in

The new troupe of Bluebells on stage between movies

New York, had instituted cine-variety shows to pad out its film programmes. A line of precision dancers was needed for the big stage, and Bluebell was approached to find them. When she had signed the contract she took with her the eleven girls fired with her from the Folies, but they were not enough for the wide Paramount stage, so their numbers were augmented to sixteen. Even then there were too few, and the producer, Jacques-Charles, after Bluebell's first Paramount show in December 1933; asked if she would mind bumping the number of girls on stage up to twenty-four.

The format of the stage show consisted of an introductory orchestral suite, played by an impressive thirty-six-piece ensemble, conducted by Pierre Millot, which would reach its climax with the curtains parting, to reveal Bluebell's line of dancers, now designated 'Les Blue Bell Paramount Girls', performing their first precision routine. This was followed by the central act — perhaps a singer, or a comedian, or an illusionist for instance — then the finale would wind things up in a spectacular fashion, usually employing a big set such as a staircase, and the reappearance of the girls following a costume change. The entire stage show would last for about twenty-five minutes, and was put on four times a day, with five performances on Saturdays and Sundays.

mount GiRLS

Every time the film programme changed a new show had to be mounted. In the Thirties the Paramount normally played its programmes for a maximum of two weeks, and if business turned out to be poor, only one week. Only in the rarest instance would a film's run be extended to three weeks. Bluebell recalls that the Gary Cooper film *Lives of a Bengal Lancer* was one such hit to be awarded a longer period. While one show was playing it was necessary for the next one to be in rehearsal, but it could not go on to the stage until the day of the first performance, which meant that the planning had to be very carefully organized. Although the Paramount opened in the mornings to show the main film feature, the first stage show was not scheduled to run until 1.30 p.m. As soon as it was finished the girls would clatter down to the basement, still in costume, where there was a large rehearsal room, its dimensions exactly the same as the stage above. There they would begin working immediately on the forthcoming show, its Music and choreography having already been determined in advance by Bluebell.

It was during this time that she stopped dancing regularly in the line and became the full-time administrator and choreographer of her team. Although she made a few subsequent appearances, particularly when Les Blue Bell Paramount Girls were featured in a few lightweight film musicals in the Thirties, she was now to adopt the role which she has fulfilled ever since.

Meanwhile at the Folies Bergère Paul Derval decided not to renew his contract with the Buddy Bradley Girls when Mistinguett's show reached its conclusion. He had been disappointed by their performance, and preferred Bluebell's style. He therefore contacted her and asked if she would like to return to the Folies for the next season's show, which he would be staging. She was happy to accept. She had seen Buddy Bradley's group in action, and while she shared Derval's critical view of them, there was one point in their favour of which she had made a careful note. Their appearance on stage was impressive on account of their height. The girls were tall, unlike Bluebell's Paramount girls, who were all around her own height, 5ft 7in. Bluebell decided that here was an attractive idea, and resolved to hire for the new Folies group the tallest dancers she could find, with a minimum of 5ft 9in. By the time the girls were costumed-out in their elaborate head-dresses and high heels the extra inches made an enormous difference, and they seemed to tower over everybody else on stage.

Consequently, Bluebell had become an impresario in her own right, for she was to continue managing the Paramount Girls, and now had her second troupe performing at the Folies Bergère. She was the direct employer of both teams of dancers. With considerable boldness she negotiated terms with Derval which she thought were audacious, but which he accepted with good grace. An association began that would last continuously for the next few years of peace, but which would be abruptly terminated with the advent of the Second World War.

The new show again starred Mistinguett, and there was also a young, horse-faced comedian in the cast, Fernandel, who in post-war years was destined to be the top French film star at the box office. Even before he had appeared at the Folies Bergère he had already made several films, some of which, such as *Le Rosier de Madame Husson*, had been successful. He was joined by an English performer and Folies favourite, Stan Randall (known to French audiences simply as 'Randall') and together they sang, danced and clowned with the voluptuous sexagenarian. For all her remoteness and self-regard Mistinguett was also a shrewd businesswoman, and appreciated that the reinstatement of the Bluebells would be of benefit to the show, although she was not going to admit it publicly. The customary iciness still prevailed, but to Paul Derval's relief there was also an acceptable state of truce, which made getting on with the production a great deal easier.

Bluebell's day was a long one. In the morning there were dance classes, rehearsals, auditions, run-throughs, sessions with music arrangers and general administration chores all calling for attention. After a hasty lunch the first performance of the day at the Paramount would begin, which would then be followed by rehearsals for the next show there. Bluebell remained at the Paramount for three of the four performances before

op: Bluebell on screen, third from left. Above: a scene from Tino Rossi's Lumières de Paris

hurrying on to the Folies Bergère in the Rue Richer, half a mile away, for the Folies performance. During the autumn months, when the stage shows at the Paramount were rested, the girls appeared in several hastily-made musical films. The Folies Bergère girls also made several film appearances, usually in lightweight musical comedies, built around such stars as Albert Préjean, Maurice Chevalier and Tino Rossi. It was necessary for the girls to report to the studios at seven o'clock in the morning for make-up and costuming, and quite often shooting did not finish until eight in the evening, giving them barely enough time to dash from the sound stages of Billancourt in the western suburbs of Paris to the theatre. Bluebell herself appeared in many of the films, but unfortunately not all of them have survived. Occasionally, however, one of these frothy confections surfaces on French television to the approval of older viewers. Of the better-known films featuring the Bluebells were *Dédé*, with Albert Préjean in 1934, Maurice Tourneur's *Avec le Sourire*, starring Maurice Chevalier in 1936, *Barnabé*, with Fernandel in 1938, and in the same year *Lumières de Paris* with Tino Rossi and *La Route Enchantée* with Charles Trenet, and finally in 1939 a romantic vehicle for Fernand Gravey, directed by Abel Gance, *Paradis Perdu*.

The Paramount had originally been built with the intention of supplementing its film programmes with stage shows, which was why there was excellent rehearsal accommodation. In the big room beneath the stage the show had to be blocked and even the dress rehearsals had to take place there. On the day of the opening of a new show, as the film programme changed, there was finally a run-through on the stage itself, at the unspeakable hour of six in the morning, for in no way was the convenience of artists to be placed above the need for the cinema to admit its paying customers, and promptly at 9.30 the doors were opened to admit those who had come for the first of the two morning film sessions. It was hard, but lucrative work, and Bluebell remained associated with the Paramount for more than three years in the mid-Thirties, for two-and-a-half of them running her dance groups simultaneously at the Folies.

From then on she not only favoured tall girls in the Folies line, but also tried as far as possible to ensure that most of them were British. It was not merely a chauvinistic gesture. Her experience had taught her that British girls had a far better aptitude for teamwork, and also for a number of odd psychological reasons were able to impress French audiences. The taboos against putting daughters on the stage were still much more deeply entrenched in France than in England, and those who made it were often of lower calibre than their equivalents from across the Channel, which was another factor influencing Bluebell's decision. In the 1935 Folies show, *Femmes et Folie*, the troupe, now expanded to twenty dancers, was billed as 'Les 20 Bluebell's Beautiful Ladies', and one of their numbers, in which the girls wore tiny feathered hats and revealing chiffon capes over sequinned

The stars of Folies en Folie, *Randall, Mistinguett and Fernandel*

pants, inspired the compiler of the programme to append the description 'Sex Appeal Aerodynamique'. A note elsewhere in the programme provided Bluebell's main credit: 'Danses anglaises reglées par MISS BLUEBELL'.

An approach was made by Mistinguett's agent to the effect that it would be beneficial for the Bluebells and for the exalted star if a troupe of the girls could appear in her new show at the Mogador Theatre. The production was nothing more than a lavish vehicle in which to show off Mistinguett, who tantalized the audience by not making her entrance until a few moments before the end of the first half, but then stayed on stage for virtually the whole of the second. Bluebell, regardless of old frictions, was happy to oblige, and the show went ahead with a team of supporting Bluebells.

There was one incident where the temperaments of the old star and the young dance director came into full collision, with Bluebell this time coming out on top. At the close of performance one night, even before the curtain had finished swishing down, Mistinguett was heard to exclaim loudly 'I would like to kill someone around here!' She then glared in a malevolent and meaningful expression at one of Bluebell's girls, before spinning on her heel and storming offstage. The following day her agent, in a hapless mood, sought out Bluebell and named the girl in question, saying that Mistinguett wanted her out of the show, and would not work in the same theatre as that particular dancer. It was nothing to do with the girl's talent on stage, but rather her activities off it. Although no reason was given, Bluebell well knew what it was. She had been going out with a handsome Brazilian dancer in the revue — but someone Mistinguett had already earmarked for

67

PROGRAMME

Left: Maurice Chevalier in the French language version of Norman Taurog's The Way to Love

Right: Josephine Baker—the Folies star who came back

herself. The girl had thus dared to become a rival to the star of the show, behaviour that was insupportable to someone of Mistinguett's stature. Bluebell had to think fast, but came up with an adroit way of defusing the tense situation that could threaten the show. She would fire the girl, she told the agent, but because she was on a run-of-the-show contract there was no way they could escape paying her the balance of her wages — she had a legal, watertight case and could sue for breach if she did not get her money in full. A scrutiny of the fine print revealed that Bluebell was absolutely right. A telephone call came from Mistinguett's agent for Bluebell that afternoon. 'Miss says you can keep her!' Bluebell had instinctively gone for one of Mistinguett's chief weaknesses, her extraordinary tightness with money, knowing that she would prefer to stomach the continuing presence of a rival rather than dig deep into her purse to get rid of her.

Bluebell recalls that Mistinguett's former lover, the great Maurice Chevalier, was afflicted with similar characteristics, possibly acquired from his mistress during the period she was training him for stardom. Perhaps more remarkably, Bluebell discovered that even though he was probably France's best-known recording star abroad, whose songs sold throughout the world, and whose thrusting lip and tilted straw hat were as famous as Chaplin's hat and cane (no less than four Marx Brothers impersonated Chevalier in their film *Monkey Business*, for instance), he had no sense of rhythm. She found out because during a season he was playing in Paris at the Empire his American choreographer asked Bluebell if she would mind going to see him privately, as he wanted to learn some dance steps for his act. Intrigued, she went backstage and after introductions were over started to work with him. She found that he was incapable of grasping a simple beat. 'He asked me if I knew what I was doing. I said, "Yes, but do you know what *you* are doing?" He had no idea. He could not even walk in tempo. All those years he really got away with murder!'

Chevalier, to her, was a superb example of the mysterious essence of stardom. The greatest performers exert such a mesmeric charm on their audiences that technical shortcomings sometimes cease to matter. Chevalier's gangling clumsiness was part of his *persona*.

'You've got it, or you haven't. No matter how good you are the public has got to care for you. A girl who has been sleeping with a producer or someone important perhaps gets an advantage, but once she's up there in front of an audience she's on her own with the public, and the advantage will go for nothing if they don't like her. I've met singers who could sing better than Sinatra, and knew it, but never got anywhere. They didn't have the thing he has. It was just the same with Chevalier. The audiences loved him!'

As the mother hen of a sizeable group of dancers Bluebell was not anxious to see her girls unemployed. But as their numbers increased it became

EN
SUPER
FOLIES

71

Backstage at the Folies Bergère, 1936

difficult to keep them all in jobs at the same time. The logical way to deal with the problem during slack periods would be to organize a touring company, and that is what, in 1935, she proceeded to do. An offer had come from Italy for a group of dancers to appear in a show starring Eduardo Spadaro, a popular comedian. So at the age of twenty-three Bluebell, having conquered the Folies Bergère and the Paramount, set out with her first travelling dance troupe and toured Italy, visiting Rome, Genoa, Naples, Bari and most of the principal resorts. The Bluebells proved as irresistible to the Italians as they were to the French, and the tall, well-built, imposing young English dancers, most of whom seemed to come from towns in the industrial north — Lancashire, Yorkshire, Tyneside — turned many heads as they made their progress around the country, travelling from place to place by train and making use of the excellent railway timetables which had proved to be the most beneficient achievement of the fascist dictator, Mussolini, in whose grip Italy was then inexorably held.

The fame of the Bluebells increased generally, and although they had appeared only on the mainland of Europe, stories about them were frequently featured in the British press, particularly in the provincial newspapers, where the presence of a local girl in the group could be counted on to enable a picture editor to brighten a dull page. In the Thirties only a

Bluebell in the line (centre) for a Thirties film

Tableau Harlem from the 1935 Folies Bergère show

handful of British people took their holidays abroad, and excursions, even to such immediate neighbours as Paris, Brussels and Amsterdam, were thought to be the prerogative of the middle and upper classes. The act of taking a Channel steamer to Boulogne or Dieppe was tantamount to embarking on an exotic adventure. It would take a world war and its aftermath to bring foreign travel to the mass population. But in the Thirties those days were still some way off. For those Britons who were fortunate enough to visit Paris an evening at the Folies Bergère was invariably high on the agenda of sights that had to be seen.

The Bluebells established themselves as favourites in Italy, and went on to make return visits. They also went to Denmark, Norway and Sweden. The European country that was carefully avoided was Germany, which since 1933 had been firmly in the hands of the Nazis. The earlier racy reputation of Berlin had been stifled by the new regime, and such frivolities as half-clad chorus girls were by necessity home-grown within the Fatherland, with a heavy emphasis on what was considered to be the Aryan ideal of female beauty.

The Nazis' disgusting notions of racial purity would have ruthlessly

74

eliminated Josephine Baker from any consideration. This luminescent half-Negro, half-Jewish American entertainer was the greatest star to be associated with the Folies Bergère after Mistinguett. She had reached Paris in 1925 after a brief singing and dancing career in the chorus line on Broadway in New York. In *La Revue Nègre*, a show which took Paris by the heels, she was its sensation. Her style of performance was something that had never been seen there before, and she immediately became the darling of the literati. Paul Derval had seen her on stage, and was as excited as everyone else. He offered her a contract to appear at the Folies. However, he paid dearly for it, both in the terms she demanded and in the anguish she caused him by her lax timekeeping, voracious sexual appetite and piratical business sense. Yet her audience appeal was so great that such disadvantages were tolerable, and her two seasons at the Folies in the Twenties were smash hits. It was then that her famous and absurd costume, consisting of a skirt made from dangling bananas and little else, was devised, becoming one of the enduring images in the iconography of titillating entertainment, to be set alongside Mae West's tight bodice and Monroe's billowing white skirt. In the Thirties, having gone on to run her own nightclubs in Europe and America, she was enjoying the comforts of stardom. Derval invited her to return to the Folies Bergère, as the star of his 1936–7 production, *En Super-Folies*, which was to run during the period of the Paris International Exposition, a world fair expected to generate tourists in record numbers.

Bluebell has far fonder memories of the warm-hearted Josephine Baker than of the icy Mistinguett. 'Josephine was quite different. Always friendly, always a word with everybody — even though she was the star!'

6   **Marcel**

IN THE HEYDAY of Bluebell's time at the Folies Bergère in the mid-Thirties, she had two groups. 'Les Bluebell's Beautiful Ladies' were all blonde and were the more energetic dancers. But there was a second line — 'Les Red Stars', whose hair was a uniform Titian red. In the 1937 show, *En Super-Folies*, Miss Bluebell's portrait appeared in the programme, with the description 'Maîtresse de Ballet', alongside a photograph of Maurice Hermite, who had written the show. On another page there was a note advising the audience that the distinctive hair colouring of both sets of Bluebells was by courtesy of 'la teinture Komol'.

The old programmes of the Folies Bergère are valuable windows on to the world of Paris by night in the Thirties. Each scene in the revue is given a title, usually along the lines of '*La Jungle Merveilleuse*', '*Soir d'Hawaii*', '*La Plus Belle Nuit d'Amour de Don Juan*', for example. Obligingly, the programmes provided translations into English, German and Spanish. There was then no necessity to cater for Japanese tourists. The Britishness of the Bluebells, who had nice lower-middle-class names like Vera, Judy, Doris, Maureen, Denise and Olwen, was in some contrast to the male dance team who, while billed as '*Les Collegiens d'Eton*', had such clearly un-Etonian names as Yves, Charlier, Jean, Nils, Maurandi and Chevrau.

The advertisements, especially, exert a powerful fascination. There was one for British Airways which depicted a nude girl in a pilot's cap dragging a bowler-hatted, monocled city gent towards a London-bound biplane, in company with several other male passengers, some clutching their briefcases, who are being lured by similarly unclad houris. The headline that went with this uncharacteristic advertisement (the British Airways of 1937 is only very vaguely related to the present-day aviation behemoth) reads: 'Toujours en joyeuse compagnie . . . sur British Airways, la ligne des vedettes' ('Always in delightful company . . . on British Airways, the airline of the stars').

The Bluebells now toured regularly and successfully. Again a group went to the Scandinavian countries — Denmark, Norway and Sweden — in addition to the resident groups at the Folies Bergère. Although in Bluebell's time he never worked at the Folies, Maurice Chevalier was to share the same stage as the girls in Copenhagen and Oslo, and the applause was rapturous. The major European country still avoided by the Bluebells was Germany, where the Nazis, having exploited the 1936 Olympic Games, which were held in Berlin, for much propaganda, were stepping up their persecution of the Jews. In his 1983 film, *To Be Or Not To Be*, which was set in Nazi-occupied Warsaw, Mel Brooks declares that 'without Jews, gypsies and homosexuals there would be no theatre', but it was these groups who suffered most from the violent and diabolical fury of the Nazis. In spite of the dubious policies of appeasement adopted by anxious politicians in other European countries, and Britain, there were no illusions in show business — Germany was an undesirable country in which to tour, unless one was blind and impervious to what was going on. There had been a massive exodus of performers, producers and directors, and indeed artists of every kind, whose work did not conform to the ideology of Nazism, and who happened to be Jewish. Not all had been able to leave, and those lucky enough to do so had to dispose of their assets too quickly to be able to get much renumeration from them. Nazi Germany was regarded with loathing and contempt by most people in the performing arts.

Race, colour and sexual tendencies have never been factors that would influence Bluebell's assessment of people. It is their talent and capabilities that have impressed her most, regardless of their personal behaviour. During her five years in Germany with the Jackson Girls she had learned to speak the language, and she still had many friends living there. Nevertheless, the regime seemed repugnant and frightening to her, and she had no desire to go back there with the Nazis in power.

As her entrepreneurial skills increased she had also grown much closer to Marcel Leibovici, whose musical skills were utilized in the Folies shows. His origins were Jewish, but he had never returned to Rumania, the country of his birth, which he had left initially to pursue his music studies in Paris when he was eighteen. Although his career as a classical musician was abandoned when he found that a steady living could be earned in the theatre, he remained a prolific composer, with some of his scores providing the backing for Folies shows, and eventually he was to lead the orchestra there. Bluebell greatly appreciated his business acumen, and came to rely on his advice and financial judgement. Their long friendship had begun in her early days at the Folies Bergère, under the nose of Alfred Jackson, when all backstage liaisons were officially forbidden, but were in fact conducted with circumspection and ingenuity. Their relationship moved through several stages as their respective careers advanced, along with their income. In 1938 Marcel at last proposed to her. Both were well-established in their professions and had good salaries with enhanced prospects. She was by now twenty-six years old, and he was thirty-four.

But there were a number of complicating factors looming. Bluebell made the alarming discovery that because of a bureaucratic quirk she would, if she married Marcel, lose her British citizenship, which she was anxious not to do. Marcel was still a Rumanian, and there were no diplomatic arrangements between the two countries to untangle the problem. The

Toujours EN JOYEUSE COMPAGNIE...

sur "BRITISH AIRWAYS"
LA LIGNE DES VEDETTES

PARIS-LONDRES
en 1ʰ20 *aller et retour WEEKEND* 490.ᶠ

BRITISH AIRWAYS Lᵀᴰ

2, Rue Edouard-VII, PARIS 9ᵉ - Tél.: OPÉRA 95-72 et 73

Airline advertising in the Folies programme

Bluebell and the girls at San Remo on an early Italian tour

lawyers set about finding a solution. There followed many months of uncertainty for the couple, who could never be entirely sure that the end result would be satisfactory to them. But at last the Rumanian embassy supplied the necessary documents to show that Marcel Leibovici was no longer one of their country's own. However, long-term domicle in France is not deemed sufficient cause to make a person French, and he had now became a stateless person. His new status, nevertheless, was sufficient to remove official barriers to their wedding.

In France a civil ceremony is required by law, but naturally enough, Bluebell wanted her union with Marcel recognized by her church. There then arose a fresh problem. Marcel was nominally a Jew, but had actually been raised without a religion at all. Bluebell, in order to marry him in church, had to make a strong case to the ecclesiastical authorities. Eventually her petition reached the office of the Archbishop of Paris, who referred it to the Vatican. The engaged couple were then summoned to see the Archbishop himself, who delivered a solemn lecture, mainly directed at Marcel. The Roman Church insisted, said the prelate, that any children of their intended union must be raised as Catholics, and that there was to be no interference by Marcel in their religious education. At the appropriate age they were to receive their first communion. It was something of an ordeal for the fun-loving Marcel to have to sit through this formal admonition, and when it was over he observed wryly to Bluebell: 'If it hadn't been for you I would never have gone through with all this!' Her rapid riposte was: 'If it hadn't been for me you wouldn't have had to!'

At long last the wedding took place. The date on which the knot was tied was 1st March 1939. Following the civil ceremony, the exchange of vows in the Mairie, before some thirty invited guests, they went on to the huge church, La Trinité, a famous Paris landmark standing in a square opposite the Rue de la Chaussée d'Antin, and close by the St Lazare railway station, where they received the blessing.

The morning's happy events concluded, the party adjourned to the Pavillon Henri IV hotel in the grounds adjoining the park and château at St Germain-en-Laye, an ancient town popular with tourists downstream from Paris along the Seine. Many of the guests, including the girls from the Folies Bergère, piled into a bus that had been specially chartered for the occasion, and followed the happy couple. At St Germain they dined on trout *meunière*, stuffed chicken, foie gras and an ice cream *bombe*, washed down with Pouilly, 1923 Volnay and liberal quantities of Heidsieck champagne. Yet there was no honeymoon. The show had to go on, and neither Marcel nor Bluebell questioned the necessity of their both being present at the Folies for that evening's performance.

The show then playing there was called *Madame la Folie*, with Jeanne Aubert as its star, and it had opened in the autumn of 1938. It had been a busy twelve-month period for Bluebell, for there had also been a number of films. One of them was *La Route Enchantée*, which was built around the sensational singing star, Charles Trenet. He had become renowned for his breezy, upbeat songs which he composed himself, and his heart-tugging ballads, the most famous being 'La Mer'. Earlier he had appeared at the Folies Bergère, but, in spite of his immense audience appeal, had incurred unpopularity with Derval, not least on account of his enthusiastic, totally overt homosexual behaviour.

In the latter part of 1938 the Bluebells had even appeared in London, at the massive, newly-built exhibition hall and indoor stadium at Earls Court, which rose up above the grey roofs of West London like a huge, concrete whale. In its early days it had been intended that the building would also house ice spectacles, and the ground floor area was designed so that the boarding could be removed and an ice rink substituted, while at the rear of the horseshoe-shaped arena a proscenium stage could accommodate scenery and dancers. Unfortunately the size and design of the hall had produced a grim, chilling place, and the great expanse of ice lowered the temperature even further, so that although outside it was a dank London November, inside the Earls Court stadium it was actually several degrees cooler, and that part of the audience in the front, most expensive, rows shivered in their fur coats. The show was not, therefore, a success.

The Folies was rapidly approaching the end of one of its most exciting eras. Derval had brought the old building firmly into the twentieth century, first remodelling the auditorium, improving both the standard of seating and the audience's sightlines, and then installing the magnificent art-deco façade

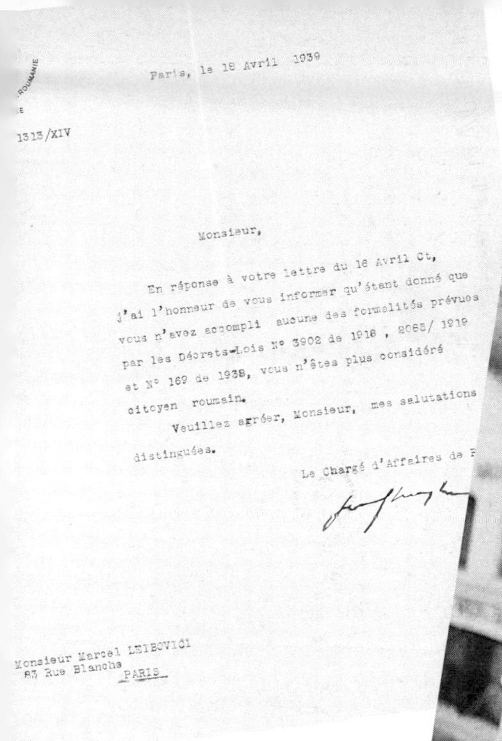

Paris, le 18 Avril 1939

1313/XIV

Monsieur,

En réponse à votre lettre du 16 Avril Ct,
j'ai l'honneur de vous informer qu'étant donné que
vous n'avez accompli aucune des formalités prévues
par les Décrets-Lois N° 3902 de 1918 , 2065/ 1919
et N° 169 de 1938, vous n'êtes plus considéré
citoyen roumain.

Veuillez agréer, Monsieur, mes salutations
distinguées.

Le Chargé d'Affaires de F

Monsieur Marcel LEIBOVICI
83 Rue Blanche PARIS

*bove: the letter that made Marcel
teless. Right: Bluebell and Marcel on
e balcony of the Rue Blanche flat.
low: the Girls at the wedding reception*

Folie en Fleurs

along the Rue Richer, which to this day remains almost unaltered. The theatre's name was sculpted in a delicate relief, in evocative Thirties 'moderne' lettering, which was etched in neon at night. Typically, the only parts of the theatre which seemed to have escaped the lavish programme of refurbishment were to be found in the part which the public never penetrated, backstage. The cramped dressing rooms, reached by steep, narrow and perilous iron spiral stairs, are still much the same as they were well over a century ago, although the graffiti on the walls will have changed. One of the most extraordinary paradoxes about the Folies Bergère is that this theatre, renowned throughout the world for the spectacular style of its sets — impressive staircases, cascading waterfalls, mirrored ballrooms — has one of the shallowest stages in Paris. The site it occupies is cramped and adjoining an ancient building that cannot be removed. Consequently, there is simply no room for expansion, and instead, for generations, the set designers have been forced to accept an additional parameter controlling their creativity, a discipline calling for great ingenuity in making every square inch of the limited space work without conveying to the audience how inadequate it really is. In contrast, the front of the house was, and still is, unusually spacious, the foyer area being as large as many an auditorium. Over the years various attempts have been made to break up the vast space, with a central bar, programme stands, seats for the intermission: none has really solved the aesthetic problem of making the scale work. During the pause in the three-and-a-half hour show the greatest crowd is invariably to be found lining up to use the theatre's only washrooms, both sexes in French style, gaining access by one door, guarded by a fierce harridan collecting fistfuls of francs from every patron who passes by her.

Unquestionably, Derval was the genius and guiding spirit behind the modern Folies, and although he has been gone for twenty years his spirit still permeates the place, as its present owner, Hélène Martini, who had bought the theatre from Derval's widow, would be the first to admit. The artistic director, Michel Gyarmathy, adheres to the Folies traditions, and retains elements of past triumphs in his shows. There are no modern stars who can make the same popular impact there as did Mistinguett, Chevalier, Josephine Baker and Damia, the extraordinary singer who was to have her own theatre named after her. As at the Lido, it is the Folies show itself that is the star. It survives as one of the last, and certainly greatest, of the once widespread Parisian music halls. There may be something anachronistic about the place, but it is nevertheless an institution, and part of the fabric of Paris. It seems that there is no shortage of people willing to pay £25 and upwards for a seat there, and on most nights of the year the house is full. With modern shows easily costing a million pounds to stage, so gone is the annual replacement. A minimum run of five years is necessary to amortize the budget. An habitué of the prewar Folies would still find things to remember, such as the stained-glass number, in which the whole auditorium

is transformed into a cathedral as concealed panels of lights are unfurled. 'Many of the effects today are the same as then,' says Bluebell. 'Only the performers are different. But a good idea remains a good idea, and can go on pleasing a modern audience, just as it would have done in the Thirties.'

Recently she returned there for the purpose of making the BBC television drama series about her life. After a search through the labyrinthine maze of passages and stairs in the backstage area she found the dressing room in which she had once spent so much time, more than fifty years earlier. Although its present occupants were absent, it being early in the day, clearly it was as active now as then, with costumes, accessories, make-up, personal trivia and belongings threatening to smother the tiny space, which amounted to little more than that obtained if two telephone booths were pushed together and given a large mirror on one wall. Bluebell entered the dismal little cell, looked round, and declared: 'It doesn't look as though they've given it a coat of paint since my time!'

During those pre-war years at the Folies from 1932 onwards she had rapidly ascended the ladder to success, having started as a mere member of the chorus, and ending as a key figure in the management of the theatre. Instead of living in the lodgings of the girl dancers at 50 Rue de Paradis, she now shared a pleasant, leased apartment with her husband in the Rue Blanche, at its northern end where it joined the Boulevard de Clichy. Here she ran various dance groups, in Paris and on tour.

It was an appropriate location for the couple, so deeply immersed in their respective show business careers. Opposite, across on the other side of the Place Blanche, was the famous Moulin Rouge, where the can-can had evolved, and the artist Toulouse-Lautrec in the Belle Epoque period had immortalized its stars, such as Jane Avril and La Gouloue, in posters that are as familiar today as they were then. The old theatre had been converted into a cinema in 1929, and the present Bal du Moulin Rouge opened up in the basement area, but the rotating sails of the windmill, one of the last of many that once dotted the slopes of Montmartre, still stood on the roof, dominating the outlook. As dusk fell delicate tracings of crimson neon outlined the shape of the sails as they gently twirled, apparently beckoning the crowds seeking their evening entertainment. By day the Leibovicis' apartment overlooked a typical Paris intersection, alive with cars, trucks and the characteristic green and cream buses on which it was *de rigueur* to stand on the exposed rear platform even if seats were plentiful within. At night the Place Blanche, which had got its name from the deposits which used to slop over from the horse-drawn carts carrying plaster quarried from

Left and below: the Folies style in the Thirties

the Montmartre hill behind, breathed an air of excited anticipation as the bright lights of the night clubs, cinemas, cafés and restaurants shone out over the traffic. For a young couple, as much in love with the music hall, cabaret and dance as with each other, there could scarcely have been a more pleasant setting, with the Folies Bergère itself only a few minutes away by taxi.

A Bluebell of the period, now a widow living in a pleasant Surrey suburb, recalls the experience of joining one of Bluebell's dance groups. She was then a fresh-faced girl from England, straight off the boat train at the Gare St Lazare. 'It was Marcel who met me at the station, and he saw me to the *pension* at 88 Rue Blanche, where many of the girls lived. It was only a few doors down the street from their apartment, and it was there that the new girls went to meet Miss Bluebell.' The induction included a stern pep talk from her — Bluebell's girls were expected to behave themselves and conduct themselves properly in the street. They were not to be seen munching things in public from paper bags, and they were required to make sure that their appearance was always up to scratch, which meant good clothes — they were always to wear hats, gloves and stockings when they went to and from the theatre. It was still an age when casual clothes were strictly for weekends in the country and on the beach, and not for strolling on the Grands Boulevards. While Bluebell was not insisting, as Alfred Jackson had done, that the girls should move in collective crocodiles, she was anxious that they should appear superior and smart, and that their reputations would always be high.

'We were sent to see the show at the Folies Bergère,' the ex-Bluebell remembered, 'where we sat in a special box. Then we were put through three weeks of arduous rehearsal on the stage there. At the end of that time we were sent by train to Italy, where we commenced our tour.' Her mother, she recalled, when she saw the Folies Bergère programme, was so incensed by the *Mannequins Nues* that she threw it on the fire, and could not be convinced that Bluebell's rules of deportment and conduct were in themselves a sound protection against the conventional pitfalls awaiting young English girls abroad. In Italy the dancers tended to rely heavily on parcels from home, containing not only valuable supplementary items of make-up, such as Leichner No. 5 and No. 9, but eyeshadow, mascara and lipstick, and pots of Crowe's Cremine, the white cream so effective at removing it all. There was also an almost unnatural craving for jars of Marmite, a dark vegetable extract unknown on the Continent, which the girls would spread on bread and biscuits before the show, believing that it would assist their stamina. Unfortunately, its manufacturers were unaware of its use in this regard, and did not therefore capitalize on it in their advertising.

The Bluebells were now as famous throughout Europe as the Tiller Girls and the Jackson Girls had been before them, and their carriage, beauty,

Above and overleaf: scenes from the last pre-war Folies show

precision and personality delighted audiences wherever they performed, thanks to the shrewd stewardship of their leader. Bluebell had reached the summit of her chosen calling entirely on her own terms while barely out of her mid-twenties, and with the astute Marcel taking an active interest in the business administration she was accorded special respect by those who had dealings with her. Although time was always precious, and both worked absurdly long hours, they realized that breathing space was needed, and were drawn to Normandy. There in the heart of the *bocage* country they found an old barn which they converted to a cottage retreat, where the pressures of the city could be momentarily forgotten, even though Paris was a mere ninety minutes distance by train. Usually, however, they would make their journeys to and fro in Marcel's powerful Citroën Traction-Avant, which he drove with ferocious enthusiasm. Once in Normandy relaxation was possible, and among the rural delights of the region an abundance of good food could be found — succulent apples and pears from the orchards, delicate wild strawberries, fresh river trout and a wide range of fluffy-textured local cheeses.

Their first child, Patrick, who was to be christened Alexandre Jacques Patrick Jean Claude, was born on 13th July, and his arrival necessitated considerable reorganization at the home in the Rue Blanche. It was not a large apartment, and one of the bedrooms was used as the office. A young

Bluebell and Marcel

nanny, Paulette Robin, was engaged and she was obliged to sleep in a bunk bed next to the filing cabinet which would be stowed out of the way during the day. Because the baby's parents were out in the evenings until very late a live-in nurse was essential, and Paulette quickly adapted to a routine which in most other households would have seemed eccentric. Bluebell has always conducted her business affairs from home, preferring to be close at hand should any domestic crisis arise, and although a succession of people were in and out of the apartment, there were many moments during the day when her full attention could be given to her young son, even, if the weather was fine, taking him to the Parc Monceau or the Bois de Boulogne for an outing.

The clouds that were forming at that time were, however, political. It was a troubled time. Since 1936 France's immediate neighbour to the west, Spain, had been riven by civil war, which had become intensified. The world had seen the results of air bombardment, and the German Führer, Adolf Hitler, had pitched lethal squadrons of Luftwaffe bombers in on the side of General Franco, the ultimate victor over the loyalist forces. The threat to European peace from a belligerent Nazi Germany was impossible to ignore, although the governments of both France and Britain steadfastly made the attempt. In the autumn of 1938, as the Armistice of the Great War was nearing its twentieth anniversary, there had been a serious possibility of a new conflict with the Hitlerian territorial demands for the German-speaking parts of Czechoslovakia, the Sudetenland, which had been annexed, as the spur, but after the Munich agreement, France, under the pusillanimous

Baby Patrick joins the group

premier, Daladier, had relaxed into complacency. The famous image of the British prime minister, Neville Chamberlain, returning from his second confrontation with the Führer, bearing his notorious scrap of paper and proclaiming that the intentions of the Germans were peaceful, generated misguided euphoria. It was short-lived; in 1939 Hitler's troops occupied the whole of Czechoslovakia. It became clear that it was a mere foretaste of the aspirations Germany had for other parts of Eastern Europe, Poland being firmly within Hitler's sights. In June the Germans signed a treaty with the Russians, a strange alliance that boded ill. Britain and France at last were united in their resolve to oppose an invasion of Poland. When the first day of September dawned Panzer divisions were already crossing the borders and airborne troops were parachuting into Polish territory. An unambiguous ultimatum was sent immediately to Berlin demanding immediate withdrawal and an undertaking to desist from further aggressive actions. Only the most optimistic spirit would have expected any heed of this message to be taken, but Chamberlain and Daladier clung as long as possible to the futile belief that war could be averted by diplomacy. In the two capitals, London and Paris, the street lights did not come on that day at dusk. The full-scale blackout, rehearsed several times before, came into effect. On the morning of 3rd September, a Sunday, Chamberlain wearily announced, in a broadcast from the Cabinet Room at 10 Downing Street, that as no undertaking from Germany had been received Britain was now at war. And France, linked by pact, concurred.

7 Deutschland uber Alles

AS FAR AS PARIS was concerned the Second World War began not with the expected big bang, but a modest whimper. At the time it did not seem so, but as the weeks went by, life gradually came back to normal after the initial shock. At the beginning there had been a general air of confusion and near-panic. The lights had gone out, and a blackout was imposed, with heavy fines meted out to transgressors. The neon lights of Pigalle and the Champs-Elysées became an evocative memory of peace. Car headlights were masked so severely that they were all but useless. The French, in any case, had been renowned for having the dimmest headlamps in Europe even before the war, there being a law that they should be amber rather than white. Gallons of white paint were splashed on trees and kerbstones to improve night-time visibility, but picking one's way around the streets in the early days of the war was a hazardous exercise, and accidents were frequent.

The call to arms was in itself a less dramatic response than that of 1914. There was a feeling that Britain had somehow brought France into the war on its coat-tails, through the reciprocal Polish pact. The plight of Poland excited far less fervour than had that of Czechoslovakia in the preceding year. Apart from the declaration of war nothing had been done to help the

Poles. Yet the words '*il faut en finir*' were on everyone's lips — the hope that they could quickly be done with it. The politicians were blamed for the diplomatic bungling that had got Europe into a fresh war, the seeds of which had been sown at the disastrous peace conference of Versailles in 1919.

There had been a general expectation that the bombers would arrive within hours of the outbreak of war, and the authorities decreed that all places of entertainment, where crowds could be expected to congregate, were undesirable and had to be closed down. The lessons of the Spanish Civil War were very fresh, and memories of the First World War, during which Paris was repeatedly shelled by a huge German cannon, nicknamed 'Big Bertha', haunted the thoughts of the public officials, who were aware that a modern aerial onslaught would make that episode look tame indeed. Shelters had been erected in various places, but not on the scale of London, where eventually entire streets of working-class houses were provided with brick and concrete bunkers.

Bluebell had already decided that all the British girls employed by her would have to be sent home, and their evacuation took place quickly and efficiently. Only two remained; they had married Frenchmen and had established permanent residence in France. There was also a handful of Germans working at the Folies, and they were allowed to leave for their homeland. With the Folies closed and her dancers disbanded an era had come to an end for Bluebell. She was still able to maintain a troupe in Italy, which had not yet entered the war, and was even then recruiting dancers to work there, but her connection with the Folies ceased. When Italy eventually came in on the Nazi side in June 1940 several of the Bluebell Girls there had harrowing experiences and had the misfortune to see the inside of Mussolini's prisons, before they were able to leave the country.

It did not take very many weeks of war for the authorities, realizing that they had over-reacted, to allow cinemas and theatres to reopen, but henceforth the hours were to be restricted. It was impossible to stage the customary new show at the Folies, and the theatre went dark, except for sporadic entertainments of a 'one-off' nature. The Leibovicis had now lost a substantial part of their income, but thanks to prudent savings and the royalties from Marcel's compositions, were able to cope. He was managing to go on working as an orchestral arranger, using the piano in the principal room. The apartment at Rue Blanche continued to be as busy as ever, and Paulette remained to take care of the baby Patrick, who was beginning to crawl with considerable agility.

This was the so-called 'phoney war', or 'sitzkrieg'. Hitler had concentrated his strength in the east, quelling Poland, and apparently still nursed hopes that a *rapprochement* could be reached with the western powers. There was an 'all over by Christmas' air of optimism prevailing on the boulevards, in spite of the general mobilization, and the presence of many uniforms, including those belonging to British officers on leave from the Expeditionary Force of Lord Gort, which was established in many of the same places that had formed the Western Front in the First World War. Hindsight has later shown that had the Allies at that time chosen to engage the Germans in an all-out attack the war might have ended there and then, since Hitler had most of his divisions on the Eastern Front.

The French had spent many millions of francs in constructing the Maginot Line, a wall of heavily armed concrete emplacements and deep bunkers running the length of the Belgian border and some way south. It was thought to be impenetrable, its vicious 'dragon's teeth' designed to tear the treads from any Panzer tank unwise enough to attempt to cross it, which would then be destroyed by concentrated machine gun fire. It was seen purely as a means of defence, and much of the French army was tied up in maintaining it. There was, it was agreed, to be no repetition of the events of the First World War, when, following the famous Schlieffen Plan, the German army broke through in the early days and got as far as the Marne, which was uncomfortably close to the French capital.

So life carried on, and the population made the best of it. Christmas came and went, but still there was no serious military activity, only the occasional German plane flying across the city on photo-reconnaissance missions, giving the anti-aircraft detachments an opportunity to practise with a live target. Initially Bluebell had wondered if she should join her girls and return to England, but had decided to stay put, knowing that Marcel preferred to live in France, and could well run into bureaucratic wrangles in Britain on account of his now murky citizenship. She, too, had fallen into the trap of complacency, and suspected that the Germans, for all their armoured might, were not going to attack France, and that Hitler's strategy would be to strike in the east, wherever he could. The war was an inconvenient punctuation in a period when things had been going extremely well; with patience it would eventually come to an end. Had she had any inkling of the course events were to take she might well have changed her mind and returned to Liverpool, with Marcel taking his chances, but as the New Year of 1940 dawned such notions seemed defeatist and inappropriate.

However, there were many people in France who believed that the Germans would win. Anti-semitism occurred in unexpected places, and Bluebell was shocked to encounter prejudice because of her husband's Jewish antecedents. The Folies Bergère had asked her to form a troupe for a new show, but, with a singular tactlessness, told her that they would prefer it if she did not come to the theatre to do so, as they were anxious not to incur the disapproval of the Germans in the event of an invasion. Bluebell recalls that the woman who made this request pointedly crossed to the other side of the street when she found Bluebell walking towards her. Shameful as such petty acts were, there was worse to come; when the Germans did eventually invade, one of the demands that they were to make was that all anti-Nazi refugees, a category that automatically embraced Jews from other

LES BLUEBELL'S BEAUTIFUL LADIES

Stella Sample

Suny Templeman

Day Gardner

Erna Otto

Maureen Goldberg

Dale Fox

Jean Lawson

Judu Spurgeon

Pris Blythe

Tessie Mc Kenzie

André Duggan

Billie Baillet

Miss Bluebell

Miss Bluebell et ses Girls

Lucy Douglas

Denise Westaways

José Newall

Lyllian Patterson

Cherry Marsh

Renée Spiller

Katherene Dunne

Hedy Wickersheim

Kitty Lind

Dot Philipps

Olwen Sudgen

Iris Crew

LES BLUEBELL'S RED STARS

countries, were to be handed over to them, with serious penalties for anyone caught harbouring such people.

It was a cold winter. Snow lay on the ground for what seemed like weeks during January and February, and the irksomeness of wintry conditions was rendered worse by the strict blackout. An unusually large number of the poor and dispossessed huddled for warmth in the passageways of the Métro. Food rationing had been introduced, and now lines of patient, waiting people were beginning to appear outside butchers' shops and in the vegetable markets.

Daladier's government of national defence believed, like Chamberlain's British administration, that the longer Hitler waited before striking the less likely it would be that such an offensive would succeed. Time was bought on both sides during the early months of 1940, but the advantage was to go to the Germans. Daladier was the first of these two premiers to be ousted. In March he was succeeded by Paul Reynaud, who conferred with the British on a plan which would seal Germany off from the Norwegian iron ore routes. Before it could be enacted Hitler's forces invaded Denmark and Norway. Now it was Chamberlain's turn to be thrown out of office. On 10th May Winston Churchill became the British prime minister. On the same day the Nazi blitzkrieg was unleashed on the Netherlands and Belgium. Rotterdam fell on the 15th and the Germans broke through across the Meuse. A brilliant tank general, Guderian, dashed forward and sealed France's fate. The expensive defences of the Maginot Line were scarcely tested. Churchill flew to Paris to find the Germans expected within days, and the government preparing to flee into exile.

Marcel, although over military age, had decided to enlist in the French army, and accordingly presented himself for medical examination. He was under no obligation to do so, not even being of French citizenship, but he was anxious to get into the fight. His call-up papers had already arrived as the fall of France became inevitable, and he never had the chance to accept the call to arms.

But before Paris was to be taken the Germans were anxious to finish off the British army, which it was now encircling. There was a brief pause in the course of the war while the exhausted Panzer divisions regrouped and replenished their supplies, giving sufficient time for the evacuation of the B.E.F at Dunkirk, a defeat that was also an extraordinary achievement. During the few days in which it lasted 200,000 British and 140,000 French soldiers, most of their equipment left behind on the beaches, were shipped across the English Channel. The remainder of the French army held off the Germans and were taken prisoner.

By the end of May a massive exodus was in progress from the French capital. Families loaded all the belongings they could on to vehicles and streamed westwards and southwards. An air of chaos prevailed. German bombers were appearing and dropping lethal loads on the suburbs; on 3rd

June 254 people had been killed in one such raid. The Citroën factory was bombed and set ablaze, and in another raid an air raid shelter crowded with women and children received a direct hit. As the residents of Paris were fleeing, so the city stood witness to the hordes of refugees from Belgium and those parts of northern France which had already been overrun, and who were passing through on their way to the south. Undeniably the war was now on in earnest.

On 11th June Paris was declared an open city, which meant that it would not be defended. It was an act that was expected to spare it from destruction. The French government was in a mood of capitulation, aware of the destruction wrought by the Nazi blitzkrieg on the great port of Rotterdam, which had been levelled to rubble. In spite of such precautions there was nevertheless great fear among the population that the bombs would shortly rain down on the densely populated inner areas. The government itself had suddenly vanished, and relocated itself at Tours, some 160 miles away. Even that move was temporary. The convoys of officials and ministers were, in a matter of days, to move on to Bordeaux.

Bluebell and Marcel had decided that they would make a dash for Bordeaux, where they had friends, with the hope, shared unfortunately by so many others, that they could find a boat to take them to England. They loaded up the Citroën, packed sandwiches and Thermos flasks of coffee, then closed up the Rue Blanche apartment and set off out of Paris. The shutters were going up throughout the city, and the roads were choked with cars, carts, bicycles and people. The road south was jammed with slow-moving lines of refugees, with many more pitifully trying to make their way on foot. Occasionally German aircraft would fly low over the pathetic columns, sending people into the ditches for shelter as machine gun bullets clattered around them. The Luftwaffe attacked on the pretext of engaging the retreating troops mingling with the tragic civilian exodus. Even when the refugees were not being strafed by shellfire and Stuka dive bombers there was desperate misery. Food became scarce and lines of hungry people besieged shops in towns along the route, even though most had long exhausted their supplies. The Nazis maintained the pressure, being at pains to demonstrate their superiority over a great nation whose morale had ignominiously collapsed. Millions of French men, women and children were now on the road, fleeing desperately from the inexorable invader.

It took five days and nights for Bluebell, Marcel, Paulette and baby Patrick to reach the outskirts of Bordeaux. The food soon ran out, and they had to make do with what little they could pick up en route. They spent nights on the roadside, sleeping in the car, during the short summer hours of darkness. Paris had fallen while they were on the road. The advance units had reached the eastern perimeter by 13th June. On the following day at five o'clock in the morning the German army began to march in. For three hours motorized columns and infantry swarmed along the boulevards, while loudspeaker vans escorted by armoured cars bellowed out their message to the remaining population. Not a shot was fired during the seizure of the city. The population of Paris at that time was normally around five million, but it was estimated that more than two million had fled, leaving the city in a state of abandonment — no newspapers, no public transport, no shops open. It was all over by breakfast time. At 9.45 a.m. the Tricolour was replaced at the Arc de Triomphe by the black, white and crimson flag of Nazi Germany, and detachments of infantry marched triumphantly down the Champs-Elysées. Two British divisions in Normandy, facing impossible odds, were evacuated. It would be four years before they were back.

It was during the humiliating fall of France that the Italian dictator, Mussolini, decided to bring his country into the war on the side of the Nazis. In view of the hysterical conditions in Italy and France it was miraculous that some of the Bluebell girls who were still working there were able to make their escape. Others were less fortunate. Their captain, Katherine Dunne, and some of the others, were arrested and subjected to rigorous interrogation before being thrown into a filthy jail in Milan. From the nature of the questioning it appeared that they were suspected of being involved in gun running to Greece, a palpably absurd and baseless accusation. The girls spent several weeks in prison, hearing of Italy's entry into the war over the loudspeaker in the cellblock. Katherine Dunne, now Mrs MacMurray, and Felicity Sands (Mrs Widdrington) recalled the ordeal. 'The food was dreadful, so was the hygiene — we had a pot in the corner of the cell for everything,' said Mrs MacMurray. 'The beds were just narrow iron bunks, four to a cell, no pillows — just a thin mattress which turned out to be full of bugs. When we woke up in the mornings we'd hear this terrible noise of beds being banged on the floor — it was other prisoners trying to knock the bugs out!' added Mrs Widdrington. After several anxious, unpleasant weeks, the only moment of exhilaration occurring when the Royal Air Force carried out a raid on Milan, the girls were suddenly released, and told that they would be deported. They were taken to the railway station and put on a train to Switzerland, under armed guard until they were across the border. In Lausanne the British Consul advised them to make their way to Lyon, which was in Vichy France, and after a hazardous cross-country rail journey from there in a jam-packed train they eventually reached Bordeaux. At the tiny port of Le Verdon they found a ship which could take them and some 2,000 other refugees to Falmouth and the safety of England. Said Katherine: 'I have always felt sorry for people locked up in prison, and I can never bear to watch a prison movie on television to this day.'

Sadly, Bluebell was unaware of what had happened, as communication was impossible. Even had she known, there would have been little that she could have done. Katherine Dunne was more fortunate than some of the girls in that she could speak good Italian and was able to enlist some help from the outside through her Italian boyfriend. When she was released she

Weekly News

Grilled By Fascist Secret Police

I IMAGINED I was being taken to the Milan police station to be asked some routine questions, the kind the Glasgow police might ask an alien visitor.

And I hadn't the slightest doubt I'd be able to answer the Italians' questions satisfactorily. After all, I hadn't done anything. My one concern was that I wouldn't be late for my lunch date with Aldo, my Italian fiance.

I got the first shock outside my hotel. Drawn up at the kerbside was a police van—a Black Maria. I stopped suddenly in amazement.

One of the detectives suddenly gripped my arm, and he and his mate bundled me into it. I found myself sitting in the back between two armed guards, ordinary police in uniform with revolvers.

"I'm being arrested!" That was the thought that kept hammering at my brain. I was wild.

"Listen, what's all this about?" I asked one of the guards.

"YOU'LL KNOW SOON ENOUGH "

 man didn't look at me. He stared ahead like one of

Head dancer in charge of a troupe on tour in Italy, Catherine Dunne was preparing for her wedding, when the Italian press began its hate campaign against Britain.

Her show moved to Milan. Then Aldo Carlo, her fiance, discovered that, under a new law, he would require special permission to marry a foreigner.

Italy made preparations for war. Catherine made preparations for home, only to be told that she could not get out without permission from the Italian Government. She made application.

Still the Italian people she came in contact with assured her Italy would never fight against Britain.

The British girl was not so sure. She discovered she was being shadowed wherever she went. Next step was a visit from two officers of the Fascist Secret Police. Catherine was ordered to "come down to the police station."

GRILLED BY

Katherine Dunne's ordeal makes headlines

could only watch helplessly as he stood on the station platform when the train pulled out, forbidden by the Fascists even to wave. She never saw him again.

Meanwhile, Bluebell and her family were unable to enter Bordeaux,

which had been closed under the weight of the refugees attempting to reach the port area. The Germans were already moving in, and permitted the evacuation to continue for a few days. The Leibovicis drew upon their savings and managed to rent a house in a nearby village, to await the time when they could get a passage. It proved impossible. Bluebell had hoped that they could try further down the coast towards the Spanish border, at St Juan de Luz, but the way there was now barred.

On 22nd June an armistice was signed at Compiègne, in the same railway coach in which the Germans had agreed the terms exacted by Marshal Foch in 1918, and which had subsequently been preserved as a national monument. Hitler stage-managed France's humiliation, and when it was over had the coach transported to Germany and destroyed.

Nevertheless, the terms could have been worse. They provided for the southern part of France, below the Loire, to remain unoccupied under a puppet French government led by the eighty-four-year-old Marshal Pétain, who had taken over following the resignation of Reynaud.

The next morning at dawn Hitler went into Paris from the airport at Le Bourget, and in a convoy of open cars he and his entourage carried out a lightning race through the silent streets, taking in a circuit of the better-known landmarks — the Opéra, the Arc de Triomphe, the Eiffel Tower, the Invalides and Montmartre — with the official photographer, Hoffman, dutifully snapping his beaming master proudly standing in famous places with the air of a tourist on a whirlwind package tour. By nine o'clock he was back at Le Bourget. It was the Führer's only visit to a city whose culture and architecture he professed to have spent a lifetime admiring.

The last boats for England left Bordeaux on 25th June. A newly promoted general called Charles de Gaulle had already escaped through the port a few days earlier, and in the absence of anyone senior had made his famous broadcast from London to the French people, telling them that they had lost a battle, but not the war. If he remained in France he would have been instantly arrested. The British, impressed by his commanding air of authority, acknowledged him as the leader of the exiled community of Free French.

Had not the remaining British diplomatic staff in France claimed the places in the last boat of all to leave Bordeaux, it is possible that room could have been found for Bluebell and her family, but instead it sailed, leaving them marooned on the edge of what was now the unoccupied zone. The Pétain government initially used Bordeaux as its capital, but aware that such a large city and port was vulnerable to attack, and in any case was, like the entire Biscay coast, part of the occupied zone, decided to re-establish itself at the small country spa of Vichy, in the heart of the de-militarized zone.

Now the dust was left to settle. Bluebell and Marcel remained at Bordeaux for nearly two months waiting to see what would happen.

The Führer's whirlwind visit to Paris

FÉRAL BENGA

4, RUE DE TILSITT (Etoile)

Tous les Jours de 17 heures à 2 heures du matin

THÉS, COCKTAILS DANSANTS

La nouvelle danse :
LE GOUMBÉ - SICCO
avec l'orchestre Africain

DINERS AFRICAINS

Le Couscous et le Riz du Sénégal

Le Fou Fou de la Guinée

Le Garry du Dahomey à la sauce enragée

Le Kanalou de la Côte d'Ivoire

CABARET - DANCING
SOUPERS
ATTRACTIONS

Chanteurs et Danseurs Africains
Leurs mélopées
Leur Tam-Tam

ORCHESTRES JAZZ-TANGO

ÉLYSÉES 73-91

Nightlife before the German curfew

Eventually, a decision had to be taken. Their funds were sinking and there were fears for the apartment at 83 Rue Blanche. They had heard in a letter that the Germans had been enquiring about it. They were now in considerable arrears with their rent, there being no machinery to transfer money, and it seemed possible that they could lose it anyway, together with the furniture and other belongings. The Germans had made much propaganda of their desire to leave Paris as untrammelled as possible by the exigencies of war, and promised to be a model occupying force. It was to be the most coveted posting for soldiers in the German army. As the summer continued people who had fled and found nowhere to go were now returning to put such claims to the test. Bluebell and Marcel were now of that number.

France had been split in two, with border posts and customs examinations separating the two zones. As Bordeaux was in the occupied area there was no necessity to have papers proving Paris residence. Bluebell felt, however, during the family's journey homeward, that already a vast bureaucratic surveillance machine had been set up, and that such movements were being carefully noted and filed. They reached Paris to find that the Rue Blanche apartment was sealed up as it had been left, and that nothing had been looted. Fears that the military authorities would have requisitioned it were happily groundless. The apartment was too small to interest them and it was to the more expensive *arrondissements*, such as the Avenue Foch area, that the army command turned to select its officer quarters.

One of the first effects of the German occupation had been the imposition of Berlin time, which meant advancing the clocks by one hour so that there was synchronization throughout Hitler's annexed territories. The chaotic conditions prevailing in June evaporated. Shops, offices, the banks and the Métro were functioning normally, although a curfew had been imposed, requiring the citizens to be off the streets by eleven p.m. unless specially authorized. The restaurants and brasseries were doing good business, catering to a new clientele, and signs in their windows announced that German was spoken. In the streets the Germans had quickly raised their own direction signs, always in German, and often in incomprehensible abbreviated military language. These wooden white arrows with their black Teutonic lettering would point towards the army's institutions and Parisians learned what was meant by '*Feldzeuglager*' and '*Hauptverkehrsdirektion Paris*' and '*Der Militarbefelhlshaber in Frankreich*'. Even hospitals were newly-designated — signs showed the way to '*Ortslazarett de la Pitié*' although it remained located on the Boulevard de l'Hôpital.

The office of the Kommandant von Gross-Paris was established at the Place de l'Opéra, and from there the new bureaucracy was set in train, with Parisians required to submit their applications for the multitude of new permits required for the carrying out of the simplest functions. Each day at noon an honour guard of the garrison, in field-grey uniforms and coal-scuttle steel helmets, would march with drums and bugles down the Champs-

Elysées, bearing the ornate standard of the Kommandantur, past the sidewalk tables of such establishments as Fouquet's and Le Colisée, where the middle-class citizens mingled with German officers in their sharply tailored tunics and peaked caps. The display served a double purpose: a reminder that orderly military rule was now controlling the city, and a ceremonial spectacle which would attract public interest.

Many famous landmarks were requisitioned for German use. One such was the W.H. Smith bookshop in the Rue de Rivoli, with its English tea-room, a popular pre-war rendezvous for visiting Britons. Predictably, under its new management it became a German bookshop. A large first-run cinema on the Champs-Elysées was taken over to become a *Soldatenkino*, showing the latest German releases, but only for the troops, who were admitted free. Other cinemas were obliged to incorporate German newsreels in their programmes and were no longer allowed to screen English films (which included American). The night clubs had reopened quite soon after the armistice, and were popular with French and Germans alike, it being customary for Parisians to remain until after five o'clock in the morning, when the curfew was lifted. The racecourses at Auteuil and Longchamps also resumed their normal role, and the enclosures were crowded with German officers and smartly dressed society women. In the initial period of occupation the Germans went to some lengths to restore a semblance of the normal life of Paris, although certain aspects of it were incompatible. It was an offence to listen to the BBC, but the French radio stations only transmitted heavily doctored news and Nazi propaganda. Newspapers, too, were heavily censored, and collaborationist publications sprang up, some taking a strong anti-semitic line. The street news stands of Paris, while no longer able to display publications from beyond the Greater Reich, carried a full range of German newspapers, including the official *Völkischer Beobachter*, *Der Adler* magazine and *Signal*, the Nazi equivalent of *Life* or *Picture Post*, which was soon to launch an edition in French.

This, then, was the Paris to which Bluebell and Marcel returned. He now lay low, going out very rarely. The Germans were requiring that Jews would have to be registered as such, an indignity Marcel had resolved that he would never suffer. He continued making a little money from music arranging, and managed to collect occasional royalties. He was able to compose using the name of a friend, who ensured that the paperwork was properly dealt with, and passed on the proceeds surreptitiously.

Bluebell was now pregnant again, and furiously resisted suggestions from well-meaning friends that, given the difficult circumstances the family now found itself in, she should have an abortion. She had worked only very sporadically in the year since the outbreak of war, mostly organizing small groups of French dancers in tiny theatres, and life was very different, although Paulette had remained to look after little Patrick.

The end of November came, and life at 83 Rue Blanche suddenly took a

Paris puts up a brave front

sinister turn. Deep in the heart of the bureaucratic machine Bluebell's name had resided. Perhaps it was inevitable that there would come a time when her file would reach the surface, and the authorities would wonder why there was this woman who held a British passport and yet had managed to escape internment. Inquiries were made with the police, who had quickly been suborned by their new masters shortly after the occupation, and were required to do much of the dirty work for the Nazi regime, working alongside the dreaded Gestapo. For the moment it was not Marcel who was under scrutiny, but Bluebell. A decision was made, a piece of paper was signed, and two members of the *garde mobile* were assigned to duty. The first Bluebell knew about it was at six o'clock in the morning of 1st December, when the doorbell of the apartment rang out vigorously, waking the entire household, and possibly most of the building, from their sleep.

105

8   Internment

WHEN DOORBELLS RANG early in the morning in occupied France it usually meant only one thing. It was the habit of the Gestapo to pounce at that time, knowing that their prey would in all probability still be in bed, and therefore particularly vulnerable. Bluebell's first thought when awakened was that they had come for Marcel. He had evaded the census of Jews which had been carried out in September, and consequently would not be designated as a non-Aryan on the official lists. Although only half-Jewish he was within the Nazi demarcation lines of Jewishness, having more than two Jewish grandparents. Patrick would have been classified as a *mischling* or mongrel, being merely one-quarter Jewish.

Yet it was not Marcel for whom the two uniformed policemen standing on the landing when the door was opened had come, but Bluebell. The policemen were young and almost apologetic. They were carrying out the orders of their masters: Madame Leibovici, they insisted, was required to present herself at the police station forthwith. They waited while she dressed and packed a small suitcase, containing the barest essentials. Most arrested people could scarcely expect such courtesy from their captors. Bluebell had no idea what was going on and questions were not encouraged.

She guessed, however, that she might be away from the Rue Blanche for some time, and tearfully bade Marcel and the baby goodbye. She was then driven off at speed to the police station, the braying siren of the car scarcely turning a head in the streets, so inured by now were Parisians to its sound. When she arrived at the police station she was told to wait with others who had been rounded up, and eventually faced a perfunctory cross-examination, the answers to the questions being carefully taken down by an impassive bureaucrat. She was aware that many Frenchmen appeared to be doing the job of the occupying Germans, and that the police station was merely a minor satrapy of the Third Reich. Eventually she was taken with other women in a requisitioned city bus to the Gare de l'Est, with armed German soldiers carefully guarding them. At the station the group was marched to a train which was standing at one of the platforms, which they then boarded. Once everyone was in place in the uncomfortable third-class carriages, with their unyielding wooden seats, keys were turned in the locks and guards stationed at salient points to discourage any attempts to escape. The old-fashioned rolling stock consisted of open coaches, each equipped with a small, over-used toilet, with no corridor connection to the next carriage.

'We were locked in for twenty-four hours on that station,' recalled Bluebell. 'Some of the women were acutely distressed — there was one old lady who must have been in her eighties. We had had nothing to eat or drink. I asked one of the German women guards if this lady could have a warm drink, but she snarled at me "Where do you think you are? Nobody gets anything here!" She was a monster.'

Eventually, on the following day, the train began moving out of the Gare de l'Est, slowly making its way through the maze of branches and sidings that surrounded all the main lines into Paris. There was no indication of their destination, although clearly they were heading south. As they reached open countryside the train began to pick up speed, but its progress was frequently slowed by signal halts, enabling other trains, carrying men and the weapons of war, to pass. The journey lasted for many uncomfortable hours, and it was nightfall by the time they reached their destination, which, in spite of the blackout, a number of the better-travelled women were able to recognize as Besançon, a town in the Doubs region, east of Dijon, and within sight of the mountains, beyond which lay neutral Switzerland.

The tired, hungry, wretched cargo of women were now loaded into a waiting fleet of battered and dusty army trucks and driven a few kilometres to the outskirts of the town. Those who were crammed in near the flaps in the canvas tops were able to see looming ahead of them the high peripheral wall of the place to which they were being taken — a barracks where they were to be imprisoned. A set of tall gates set in the wall swung open to allow the small convoy of trucks to enter. Beyond the guard house were serried rows of barrack blocks, lately the residence of part of the French army, but now taken over and re-designated as an internment camp for those persons likely to cause trouble to the occupying Germans. There were many thousands of men imprisoned there as well as the women, and their compounds were separated by walls and armed sentries.

Bluebell had been picked up and brought to this place because she carried a British passport, and therefore in the eyes of the authorities was an enemy alien. It was the fate that had befallen a number of other Britons who had been stranded following the fall of France. Clearly, those in the uniforms of the armed forces would be held as prisoners of war, but the position of civilians was different. Some had by various means achieved repatriation through neutral countries, but the majority were less fortunate, and found themselves being held in camps such as the one at Besançon, where conditions were generally unpleasant. Similar roundups of enemy nationals had occurred in the United Kingdom, and many Italian restaurateurs, Bavarian delicatessen proprietors and Viennese musicians found themselves behind barbed wire enclosures in the Isle of Man. Therefore there was nothing unusual in the circumstances of Bluebell's arrest. She was, however, now several months pregnant, and was not above using her condition to exert some pressure on the camp administration.

The women were allocated to the various barrack rooms, each of which held eighteen of them in ungenerous spaces that contained an iron bedstead and a small locker. The only source of heat was a wood-burning stove in the centre of the room. As soon as Bluebell spotted it she declared: 'Let's all have a nice cup of tea!' Her cheerfulness was an immediate boost to morale, and the women set to, attempting to make the best of a very depressing situation. Somehow they got through the first night, reinforced by the first hot meal since they had been arrested and placed aboard the train in Paris.

At what to Bluebell must have seemed an unreasonably early hour they were wakened and told to get themselves in order. A uniformed German woman entered the room and addressed them in excellent English. She explained that they would be expected to fend for themselves as much as possible, which meant that each room would be responsible for food preparation, cleaning, washing-up, laundry and general chores. It was made clear that they had not been sent to a holiday camp. A duty roster was drawn up and the various functions under it allocated. Bluebell then announced that she was not going to participate. The other women were astonished. They said that she would never get away with it, and how could she possibly justify such an attitude. 'Because I don't do these things at home,' said Bluebell. 'But you are not at home,' said the German woman. 'That is not my choosing,' Bluebell replied. The others shuddered, expecting her to be taken out and shot, or at least thrown into a windowless dungeon. Instead the woman turned on her heel and walked out of the room, unwilling to be further drawn into what had become an unwinnable argument.

It was characteristic of Bluebell constantly to push her luck with the

Barracks at Besançon—transformed into internment camp

Germans, often to what to observers seemed an almost foolhardy degree.
But the years that she had spent in Germany had not been wasted. Apart
from learning the language, an asset which she purposely did not advertise,
she had gained valuable insights into the Teutonic psyche. She was aware
that great importance was attached to the proper way of doing things and
that Germans hated unconventionality and also weakness. She knew that if
she spoke strongly, confidently and uncompromisingly they would back
down rather than become involved in an altercation. It was also clear to her
that none of the others, many of whom were middle-class Englishwomen
who had been to boarding school, and were trying to make the best of things,
would pluck up the nerve to try it.

'Not for one moment did I ever think that there was any possibility that
Germany could win the war,' she says. 'I believed that, and if I hadn't, it
would have been a different story.'

The others therefore went off to work at their various duties, but Bluebell
remained behind. Some of the women resented her getting off heavy chores,
but the majority admired her spirited refusal to be pushed around by the
Germans. Bluebell was also scornful of the medical facilities offered in the
camp, and demanded to be seen by a civilian gynaecologist. Again the
Germans, amazed at her audacity, capitulated.

While she was at Besançon she found herself in the curious position of
being able to communicate, via letters passed on by the Red Cross, with
Aunt Mary in Liverpool, but not with her husband in Paris. She attempted

to smuggle letters to him out over the wall, but to no avail. Nevertheless, efforts were being made on her behalf which at the time she did not know about. Marcel had gone to the Irish Legation in Paris following Bluebell's departure from the Gare de l'Est. There he found a sympathetic Frenchwoman called Madame Froc, who noted the details of Bluebell's birth. Later, she wrote to the Irish Chargé d'Affaires, one Count O'Kelly, and offered the opinion that if papers were produced to the Germans proving that Bluebell was born in Dublin, and therefore an Irish national, then they would have no cause for holding her, as she was a neutral and a non-combatant. The question of her possession of a British passport was easily explained — anyone born in Dublin before the establishment of the Irish Free State in 1921 would be quite likely to hold a British passport, as prior to that time Great Britain was the sovereign power. Many Irish nationals had not bothered to exchange them for the document issued by the government of Eire, not least because the British passport before the war carried considerably more weight than those issued by smaller countries.

Count O'Kelly, who had already succeeded with that ploy in other instances, took up the case. When he learned that Mrs Leibovici was a good Catholic who was expecting her second child, and that it could be proved easily that her birth was registered in the Irish capital, he resolved not to let the matter rest until she was returned to her home. But there were various bureaucratic procedures to be undertaken before Bluebell could be released. Meanwhile, she was obliged to spend a miserable Christmas at Besançon. Eventually, she was told that an intercession had been made, and that she would be allowed to go back to Paris. She was released from detention on New Year's Eve, accompanied by three Sisters of Mercy who had also been freed, and whose vast, tent-like white cowls attracted considerable attention.

At the railway station a note of farce intruded into what should have been an occasion of some seriousness. The women had been duly driven there according to official instructions and deposited in time for the Paris train. The truck had then driven away, leaving them alone and unguarded for the first time since their detention. At the barrier their tickets were demanded for inspection. They said that they had no tickets. They were invited by the railway official who was overseeing the gate to the platform to go and buy them at the ticket office. The women explained that they had no money either. No tickets, no travel, they were firmly told. The nuns, having already endured much hardship, began to weep.

Bluebell exploded with rage at the thought of her homecoming being delayed by some pettifogging bureaucrat. 'We have just come out of that terrible place,' she said, 'and we have no intention of going back there. Get on the phone to them,' she ordered, 'and tell them that if they do not pay our fares we shall personally take the station apart.' By this time the stationmaster had been summoned to deal with what was developing into an unseemly row, and he put a call through to the administration office at the camp. A profuse apology was given by the official there who had forgotten to issue the necessary travel warrants, and the matter was settled just in time to allow the ex-detainees to take their place on the fast train which would be going straight through to Paris.

She reached home just in time to see in the New Year of 1941, scarcely an occasion of great celebration, since the war had for sixteen months been going entirely Germany's way. Much of Scandinavia, the Low Countries and France had been invaded, and there seemed to be no prospect of the British being strong enough to mount a counter-attack at that stage of the war, the scars of the humiliation of Dunkirk being too recent. The Battle of Britain had been fought, and the Royal Air Force had successfully held off the opening stages of a German invasion, forcing Hitler to shelve his Operation Sealion, as the plan was called. But now the heat was on London, followed by other major cities, including Liverpool, which were being pounded night after night by the heavy bombers of Goering's Luftwaffe, with the RAF and the ground defences at that time having insufficient resources to hit back. Bluebell had no way of knowing whether Mary Murphy had survived the raids or not, and the Nazi-controlled Paris radio suggested that few buildings were left intact on Merseyside after the bombers had carried out their grisly task. She had a small radio which was able to receive the BBC transmissions from London very clearly, and although listening to such broadcasts was against the law, she depended on that source for accurate, although carefully censored, war information. Just as the German propaganda machine would try to give the impression that the British cities that had been attacked had been destroyed, so conversely the authorities in London played down the bombing to avoid giving helpful information to the enemy.

The reunion with Marcel and Patrick, who had been looked after while she was away by Paulette, was joyous. But it was now a time to walk very carefully. The Germans were beginning to tighten their grip on the Jewish population in Paris and many who had not registered according to the new law were denounced by informers anxious to collect the few francs offered by the authorities.

Marcel decided that Paris was becoming too uncomfortable, and rather than risk a further arrest in the family, with possibly fatal consequences, he felt that it would be better to make his way to the unoccupied zone in the south, where there were many contacts. It was getting too dangerous for him to go out on the streets, as random checks, in which the police stopped people to inspect their papers, were becomingly increasingly frequent. To be unable to produce the correct documentation was to risk instant arrest, which as often or not would entail investigation by the Gestapo. Once his Jewish antecedents had been established he would be in serious trouble for failing to register. So he remained at home, writing music which would be

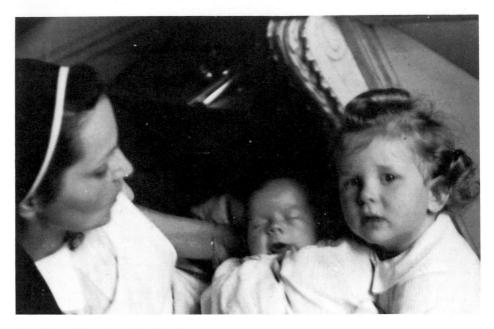

Patrick and Francis and a friendly nun

ascribed to a non-Jewish friend. The ensuing royalties, while not the same as a regular income, at least brought some money in.

He decided that he could be of more use if he were in the south of France, in the zone that was then ruled by the Vichy government, where he had many friends, and where he would be able to move around with more freedom. After a period of planning and discussion he quietly slipped away. However, it was not until weeks later that Bluebell finally received a message that after having made several pauses in his hazardous journey, including a stay of three weeks in Montpellier, he had reached the great Mediterranean port of Marseilles.

Although the new year of 1941 was generally gloomy for everyone except those who supported the Nazis, there was, however, one happy event in the lives of the Leibovicis. On 19th April, six weeks before Marcel's departure from Paris, Bluebell's second child was born. It was another boy, and he was christened Francis Kelly Alain Michel. In spite of the now acute food shortages Bluebell and Paulette took care to see that he did not lack essential nourishment, and Patrick, now nearly two years old, was delighted with the new addition to the family, although initially he had been hoping for a sister.

The war continued to go badly for the Allies. The beat of the Luftwaffe had extended from London to the great provincial industrial bases of England, and nightly raids on such cities as Coventry, Liverpool, Plymouth and Southampton were triumphantly described by Radio Paris. In the desert of North Africa Hitler's soldiers, under the brilliant, dashing leadership of Field Marshal Rommel, were routing British forces and advancing steadily on Cairo and the great prize of the Suez Canal which lay to the east. In Yugoslavia and Greece the Germans met with fierce partisan resistance, but the sheer might of the Wehrmacht brought these countries under the control of the Reich. In June came one of the biggest surprises of the war, the launch of an all-out attack by the armies of the Third Reich on the Soviet Union. The self-confidence of the Nazi war machine was staggering — Russia was not only a vast country, but had a huge population compared with that of Germany, and could muster a seemingly endless number of defending troops. Overnight, the Russians ceased to be the dreaded Stalinist Bolsheviks, and instead were hailed as heroic allies. And it seems likely that the day in 1941 when the Germans launched Operation Barbarossa, as the eastern onslaught was designated, was also the day on which Hitler ensured that Germany would eventually lose the war.

The mood in Paris changed perceptibly. The various factions became polarized, so that broadly the collaborators and supporters of the Vichy government were of the Right, and the Resistance, or underground, became the preserve of the Communists. Many Frenchmen of Fascist leanings were induced by the Germans to enlist in the fight against Bolshevism, and, spurred by good pay and rations, joined Gallic units of the Wehrmacht to go to the eastern front.

Anti-semitism became more fanatical. In September the Nazis opened a big exhibition at the Palais Berlitz, *Le Juif et la France*, which set out to prove both an organized conspiracy between the Jews and the Communists to achieve world domination, and the racial degradation and criminality of the so-called inferior peoples. A million Parisians lined up to see it.

Without Marcel, and with two little boys to feed and Paulette to support, Bluebell was beginning to find the going increasingly hard. She was unwilling to return to work at the Folies Bergère, even if Derval had offered her a job, in view of the attitude he had taken towards Marcel as a Jew. In any case, the theatre was now largely patronized by the Germans, who regarded a visit there as the highspot of an exotic leave in the French capital. Leaving Paris for the country did not seem a wise option in view of her pronounced British accent, which in a small rural town would draw immediate and unwelcome attention, but which seemed much less noticeable in Paris, where there was a sizeable population of immigrants to whom French was clearly not the mother tongue. So, as life became harder, she remained in the capital, and waited for something to happen.

An opportunity was to arise. In the summer of 1941 she was approached, out of the blue, by a theatre manager she had not previously known and asked if she would like to put a show on in a little cabaret in the Rue Fontaine, only two hundred yards from her apartment in the Rue Blanche. Bluebell accepted the invitation. The theatre was called the Chantilly, and its patrons were mainly French, rather than the German military occupiers of Paris. It was probably the sort of place that a respectable German would have regarded as being unworthy of his patronage, preferring the more sophisticated and famous night haunts. 'I never ever saw a German uniform there,' said Bluebell, 'and if they did come they would have worn civilian clothes.' The tiny stage could only contain ten dancers, and she had no difficulty in hiring the required number from her large circle of contacts in Paris, all French but for two British girls who had married Frenchmen.

The performances were scarcely in the same league as the Folies, with minimal scenery, a three-piece musical accompaniment rather than a full orchestra, and costumes that were cobbled together from precious scraps of hoarded and recycled material. The shows, in common with all entertainments in Paris, had to be finished by 10.30 in the evening in order to allow customers time to beat the eleven o'clock curfew. During the occupation people who had gone out in the evening would be obliged to stay put until the following morning if they were caught in the curfew, and it was customary for some of the night clubs to retain a sizeable number of patrons until past 6.30 a.m. on the next day.

It appeared that the clientele at the Chantilly, while not German, was very definitely shady. It was a favourite haunt for black marketeers, who would openly conduct their transactions over drinks. There was also a number of showgirls who paraded on the stage and then later mingled in a friendly fashion with the audience, but they were kept entirely separate from Bluebell's team. 'I've never allowed my girls to do that — ever! It is something that they simply do not do,' she insists firmly. But even Bluebell herself was one night approached backstage by the sheepish owner of the Chantilly to say that he had been asked to give her an invitation to go to a table, and to sit with a prominent official. He had, it seems, shunned the other girls offered him, setting his sights instead on 'the English girl who is hidden behind the curtain'.

She had always taken great care that the audience would not be aware of her presence, and was astonished that her attempts to remain hidden were of such little avail.

Bluebell also recalls that one evening a faction of 'Darlanists', the right wingers who supported the French quisling, Admiral Darlan, descended on the place, and a roughhouse ensued, followed by gunfire as the rival gangs of collaborators and black marketeers fought each other. Bluebell rounded up her girls and kept them out of sight backstage, while the regular customers who were not involved in the gun battle dived under the seats for protection. It all ended as suddenly as it had begun, with the arrival of the police, who then set about arresting as many members of the opposing sides as they could. When order was finally restored the Chantilly was officially closed down and its doors securely fastened with padlocks. But the ban was short-lived. It lasted for only three days, following which time the

The smaller scale of the wartime line

establishment was restored to business, in all probability after appropriate financial transactions had been engaged in between the proprietor and the police. It was said to be the only way that places such as the Chantilly could remain in business.

In spite of the relative absence of Germans at the theatre, it became clear to Bluebell that they were well aware of her activities. One day she received a telephone call at the Rue Blanche requesting that she take herself off to the Empire and present herself to a certain Colonel Feldman. The Empire had become one of the centres of the rest and relaxation business in Paris, and Feldman, seated behind an enormous desk, and flanked by a pair of husky soldiers acting as his bodyguards, turned out to be nothing more sinister than the Third Reich's booking agent for theatrical turns.

He was, he explained to her, impressed with her show at the Chantilly. Bluebell noted that on his desk was a fairly thick dossier bearing her name, and began anxiously to wonder what all the information that had been gathered on her could be, and who had been responsible for acquiring it. Feldman then went on to say that he wanted her to go to Germany, to Berlin and elsewhere, and to stage the same show, which he assured her would be very much welcomed by the troops. She would, he assured her, be well looked after, handsomely paid, and given ample rations and an excellent apartment. Bluebell, aware that many French entertainers had been lured down this path, including Maurice Chevalier, said that she could not even consider it. 'Why?' said Feldman. 'You are Irish, a neutral!'

'That may be so,' said Bluebell, 'but I have a British passport, and I am a British subject. I have many relatives who are soldiers and are fighting against you Germans. You must understand why I cannot for a moment contemplate entertaining your troops!'

The colonel mused for a moment, considering the adroit argument that had been presented to him. Bluebell had wisely chosen to appeal to his sense of military decorum. 'Quite so, madame,' he said, and politely brought the interview to a conclusion. She never heard from him again.

There was, however, a disquieting item of information for her early in the new year of 1942. It was relayed to her by various contacts, who used the unorthodox methods of communication that had sprung up to substitute for the old heavily censored mails. In Marseilles, she was told, there had been one of the periodic police round-ups, and Marcel had been taken in, no doubt because his forged papers had been detected. Worse, his Jewish antecedents had been revealed, and consequently he had been sent to a special internment camp for Jews, at Gurs in the Basses-Pyrénées, which for many unfortunates was to be a staging post on the way to the death camps of Germany.

 In Hiding

THE NEWS THAT MARCEL had been taken by the Germans was distressing. But Bluebell carried on, hoping that some miracle would happen. She had no illusions about the dangers now faced by millions of people in France. Denunciations followed by disappearances were becoming commonplace, and it became increasingly difficult to find anyone whose trustworthiness was absolute. The reward paid by the Germans to anyone giving away a Jew was 100 francs, which was a modest sum for a human life. There were some who made it a profitable trade, particularly when they were able to denounce whole families at a time.

Although in December 1941, following the Japanese attack on Pearl Harbor, the Americans had at last entered the war, the mood in Paris had hardened rather than softened. Hope now stirred in the souls of a few, who realized that the resources of the United States could now be called upon to create a war machine that would ultimately defeat the Nazis. Hitler had been heavily stretched since the war had been taken to the eastern front, in spite of the skill of the Panzer commanders, and the fighting was becoming increasingly savage as the Russians fiercely defended their homeland, showing the most extraordinary courage in the field as the casualty figures

117

of their forces and civilians soared into millions. Bluebell had never belonged to the group of French people who had accepted the occupation as inevitable, but had always firmly believed that the presence of the Germans was temporary. After Pearl Harbor she knew that it was only a question of time, and that patience would eventually pay off.

In Paris the polarities intensified. The persecution of the Jews was stepped up, and the first sad trainloads left for Auschwitz, carrying men, women and children in sealed cattle trucks from Drancy, the large concentration camp that had been set up in a half-finished housing project close to Le Bourget airport, and alongside a convenient railway line. In May 1942 an order came into force compelling Jews to wear a six-sided yellow star with the word '*Juif*' in its centre when they were on the street, a practice that was already in use in Germany and in other occupied countries. Had the Rue Blanche flat the Leibovicis had lived in since before the war been owned by them, instead of rented, it could have been seized as Jewish property, but as it was not recorded as such it remained untouched.

Bluebell, in spite of the risk, did not hesitate when a dishevelled young woman came one night to her apartment, and told her that she was a Rumanian cousin of Marcel's and had escaped from the Germans, who had come into her Jewish neighbourhood with the intention of rounding up whomever they could. She had been able to get away by climbing through a lavatory window. It was a side of Marcel's family that he rarely had any contact with, but the girl told her that she was the daughter of Marcel's aunt, and was a university graduate and a qualified pharmacist. She begged Bluebell to shelter her. The harbouring of Jews was an offence that carried the death penalty, and frequent warnings to this effect were broadcast on the Nazi-controlled Radio Paris, but Bluebell hid the girl in the small apartment until she had been able to obtain convincing false papers, and could venture out more easily.

The streets could never be safe. On a sunny day the two women were stopped by a couple of young men as they strolled along the Boulevard Haussmann. At first they thought that they were '*zazous*', a breed of rootless, mannered, youthful layabouts who infested the cafés and bars, wearing dark glasses and drainpipe trousers. However, it quickly became apparent that they were special policemen.

'Show us your papers!' demanded the elder of the two. 'No, you show me yours!' answered Bluebell. He produced a police identity card indicating that they were indeed official. Bluebell's documents were carefully scrutinized, including the letter which had got her out of the camp at Besançon. Eventually they were returned to her, and she was told she could move on. She made to wait for her companion, but the girl said quickly to Bluebell: 'You had better go — I'm in trouble.'

It seemed that one of the men, who had a very keen ear, had detected a Rumanian cadence in the woman's voice, in spite of her educated French accent. When he challenged her with being a Rumanian she had denied it. They decided that as she had a French identity card that made no mention of foreign origin she should be taken in so that her papers could be looked at more closely. She was brusquely bundled into a nearby vehicle and driven away, under arrest, leaving Bluebell standing on the street. It was the last time Bluebell was to see her.

She returned home in a thoughtful mood. The chances were that the girl would be intensively interrogated and probably tortured to make her reveal who her contacts were, once the forged papers had been detected. Even some of the toughest members of the Resistance had cracked under the treatment meted out during such interviews. There was no way that she could be rescued. But there was every chance that Bluebell would be the next to be arrested, and undoubtedly would face a long sentence, if not execution, for hiding a Jew. There was nothing in the flat to indicate that the woman had been there — she had arrived with only the clothes she was wearing, and her handbag, and subsequently had borrowed additional garments from Bluebell.

After many nerve-wracking hours they came for her. They chose the customary hour to make their swoop, six o'clock in the morning. The doorbell rang and Bluebell found found two French policemen and a German in Gestapo uniform demanding admittance. The girl, by now in Drancy, had confessed, and denounced Bluebell, as well as another woman who had been responsible for supplying the false documents. Bluebell stoutly asserted in the face of vigorous questioning that she had never seen the young woman before, and that she had been accosted by her in the street only a few moments before they were stopped for their papers to be checked. The police searched the apartment from top to bottom but could find nothing incriminating.

'I don't know,' said Bluebell, 'how I could lie so convincingly. I think it was because we were living under such tension then that life and death were almost unimportant. I was lucky, too, in that I wasn't taken to the prefecture. The woman who had supplied her with the false papers was taken there, and she was never seen again. I heard afterwards that she had been shot.'

Bluebell's vehement denials were apparently convincing enough to satisfy the police and they went away, never questioning her again about the incident. Meanwhile, she learned from sources that were tapped in to Drancy that the girl was later transported to a German concentration camp and almost certain death.

Marcel was to be more fortunate. The camp at Gurs was a large one, consisting of rows of wooden barrack blocks divided into various compounds and surrounded by a perimeter fence with watchtowers and guards. It had originally been built in 1939 to house refugees who had fled from the Spanish Civil War. The prisoner population was almost entirely

119

Jewish, and the inmates were mostly of foreign origin. In October 1940 13,500 German Jews had been sent there to add to those who had come from all over France and every walk of life. More than a thousand of them died within two months from disease, mostly typhoid and tuberculosis, because conditions were so bad. There was also much promiscuity, as men, women and children were crammed together in their huts, with little or no privacy. Initially, because Gurs was in the unoccupied zone, it was run by the local gendarmerie, with Spanish refugees working in the camp offices. In 1942 the Germans took over, and began sending prisoners to Auschwitz from mid-August.

Marcel found that he was not wanting for artistic company, as many other musicians had been interned with him. There were also a number of artists and, surprisingly in view of the shortage of sustenance, ink and paper was available. There were even art classes, run by the inmates, and drawings made in the camp are still in existence, providing an authentic record of life at Gurs.

But every week there would be a hut inspection, and almost every time an SS officer would call out the names of certain prisoners, who would be told to get ready for transfer to another camp. These were the selections for Auschwitz and other concentration camps in Germany, and most of those culled from the huts at Gurs in this fashion were never heard of again.

It soon became known that Marcel's knowledge of the German language was excellent, and he became in demand as an interpreter. As a result he was able to communicate much more freely with his jailers than could the other prisoners. In time he acquired certain privileges denied the others, the most extraordinary one being that he was allowed to accompany the food truck on its trips out of the camp into the nearby town. There was considerable opposition within the local community to the sale of food to the camp, where many of the inmates could only subsist on parcels sent in by various relief agencies such as the Quakers and the Red Cross.

The Germans asked Marcel to translate for them in dealings with the local tradespeople, who were not averse to taking advantage of language difficulties if it meant that they could make some profit from the camp commissariat, the Germans finding themselves less able to bargain than they would have hoped. Marcel did his job conscientiously, savouring the free air and occasionally nibbling at fresh fruit before it was delivered back to the camp kitchens for distribution among the multitude of inmates. He knew, however, that it was only a matter of time before he, too, would be transferred to a harsher concentration camp, as Gurs was really a vast holding station, and few prisoners were likely, once the deportations had begun in earnest, to remain there for more than a matter of months. But the regular routine of the German shopping expeditions had not gone unnoticed in local quarters.

Marcel had a longstanding and remarkable friend, another musician,

Gurs: the camp conditions, and Marcel, drawn by a fellow inmate

called Guy de la Morenière, who was not Jewish and had been able to continue living in Paris. They had first met when they were fellow students in the early Twenties at their musical academy, the Schola Cantorum in the Rue St Jacques. Guy had by now become a shadowy figure with many underground contacts. Periodically he saw Bluebell and passed on news that had travelled along the grapevine. He had heard from Gurs of Marcel's regular excursions from the camp, and realized that they presented an opportunity for escape. So he worked on producing a false identity card for Marcel, and one day he requested from Bluebell a suit of Marcel's clothes, without offering any explanation as to why he should need them. She could only guess.

Armed with these items Guy made the journey into south-west France, crossing the various checkpoints without incident. The escape was astonishingly easy. Marcel had won the trust of the German soldiers on the shopping detail, and their vigilance was perfunctory. The operation had been carefully pre-arranged through Guy's contacts with the local Resistance group. It was a relatively easy matter for Guy to wait for the arrival of the truck in the market place, then quickly tell Marcel to give them the slip, while the driver and guard were having a quiet rest and a cigarette. Marcel ducked behind the scenes in a shop and, out of sight of the Germans, quickly changed into the clothes brought by Guy.

Calmly the two men made their way out of the sleepy town, and hid in fields until nightfall, then made their way under cover of darkness to the next town, Pau, where there was a railway station. There they were able to board a train without being challenged, although Marcel's absence would certainly have been noted. It is possible that his escape was initially covered up by his German escort, since it had occurred through his negligence on a scale which would have called for a court martial.

They had to change trains during the course of the journey and carefully covered their tracks by obtaining fresh tickets, thus disguising their point of origin. They passed through various checkpoints along the route, but the papers were drafted well enough to arouse no suspicion. Eventually they reached Paris and Guy took Marcel to 37 Rue de la Boucherie, where there was a small, but convenient, sixth-floor attic which he leased but did not occupy. It was to becomes Marcel's hideout for many months and the location had a certain piquancy in that directly across the street stood the buildings of the Prefecture of Police, the police headquarters. From there frequent raids were launched to flush out other persons-in-hiding, but the police never conducted their searches on their immediate doorstep.

Guy advised Bluebell of Marcel's presence in Paris, to her great excitement. She began a task that was to last for the next two-and-a-half years, ensuring that her husband should receive food, have his washing and mending done, and be supplied with reading material and manuscript paper to allow him to while away the long, boring hours. Leaving the attic was out of the question, particularly during the summer months when daylight extended almost to the hour when curfew began. Marcel could not be permitted to have a piano, since its sound would be heard across the rooftops and might invite interest. It was a dismal incarceration, but it was infinitely preferable to being holed up in the camp at Gurs.

Finding sufficient food without a ration card for Marcel was an additional problem. Bluebell had a good contact, a man called Frederic Apcar, who lived on the western outskirts of Paris, at Vaucresson. Before the arrival of the Germans in 1940 she had wisely bought a bicycle, realizing that other means of getting about were likely to become difficult. The bicycle now became supremely important. There were very few cars, other than official ones, still on the streets, and many of the buses had been requisitioned for war purposes. Those that remained were crowded, infrequent and mechanically unreliable. Only the Métro functioned with anything resembling its pre-war efficiency. The Lcibovicis' own Citroën had remained in a garage a few doors down the Rue Blanche, jacked up off the floor and rendered useless.

Bicycles had become enormously valuable and new ones were hard to find. Theft was commonplace, in spite of the registration plates they had to carry. It is thought that by the time of the liberation there were more than two million of them in Paris. People were prepared to pay as much for a bicycle as they would formerly have considered an appropriate sum for a car. Even the cab trade had gone over to pedal power, and enclosed *vélo-taxis*, variations of the bicycle rickshaws of the Far East, were the main method of transportation for the better-off citizenry of Paris.

Bluebell used her bicycle to visit Frederic Apcar each week in order to purchase food supplies, which he in turn bought from Poles working on the farms. Every few days she would cycle over to the Rue de la Boucherie with food and other items hidden in the deep basket slung across the handlebars. On one occasion during the long ride from Vaucresson she cut the curfew time too closely, and was stopped by a pair of gendarmes who asked her what she was doing. She made some excuse about a sick relative and waited for them to inspect her basket. Fortunately they did not do so, but gave her a gentle ticking-off, explaining the dangers of breaking curfew. 'On your way, madame,' they said, 'and if you are stopped again, remember. We haven't seen you!'

After Marcel had been living in the attic for a few months, Guy's office was raided, following a tipoff from an unknown collaborator. There was only a girl typist there at the time, but she was taken into custody. Guy rang Bluebell at six o'clock in the morning, and told Bluebell that it was necessary to get Marcel away from the attic as soon as possible, as the authorities now had the address, and it would be only a matter of time before they followed through with another raid.

Bluebell acted fast. She knew a woman who owned an empty apartment in the Rue Bertholet on the Left Bank, and she agreed to let Bluebell have it. The concierge, a delightful elderly woman, was both helpful and kind, and readily agreed to look after the new tenant. So Guy and Bluebell quickly made the transfer, getting Marcel out of the attic and down the street, hoping that no police observers were watching the door. Within the hour Marcel was installed in his new quarters.

Once again Bluebell had become pregnant. She was determined to have a family and felt that with her career undergoing a temporary lull the time was auspicious. It meant that she would have to leave the Chantilly to get on by itself for a short period. The war news seemed to be improving — she had heard over the the the BBC how the British 8th Army had broken through at El Alamein, and were now driving the Afrika Korps westwards. There was talk of a Second Front launched by the Allies, which would be the start of the liberation of Europe. The Nazis had engaged hundreds of thousands of Central Europeans as slave labour for the notorious *Organisation Todt*, and were using them to construct massive concrete fortifications along the north-west French coasts, the so-called Atlantic Wall which Hitler believed would be strong enough to repel any invasion attempt. Many Frenchmen in the engineering and construction industries supplied their design expertise and management for these defences, and thus not only prospered from collaboration with the Germans but impeded the liberation of their country. Not all of them were brought to justice after the war.

The landing of American forces in French North Africa brought about an immediate suspension of the unoccupied zone as a retaliatory action, and Vichy France became absorbed into the rest of the country, with the Germans taking charge. It was further indication of the uneasiness that the Nazis were feeling with the progress of the war.

Bluebell experienced a further close call. In July 1943 a brusque telephone message to the Chantilly ordered her to present herself to the Gestapo headquarters at 84 Avenue Foch on the following morning. Such invitations, which could not be refused, often resulted in the arrest, detention, torture and execution of the unfortunate recipients.

'I went because I had no choice,' said Bluebell. 'Had I tried to get away from Paris I would have been quickly spotted with my English accent. There was nothing else that I could do.'

The building was a large mansion on the most magnificent of the avenues radiating from the Place de l'Etoile like the spokes of a wheel. It had become one of the most loathsome places in Paris, and many loyal Frenchmen had died in its basements and torture chambers. But as Bluebell presented herself she was only aware of uniforms and filing cabinets, telephones and typewriters, the trappings of a military bureaucracy occupying what had formerly been the lavishly furnished salons of an elegant building.

She was ushered into an office on the second floor where a distinguished-looking officer was seated behind a desk, with, in the customary fashion, an

Nostalgic yearnings for better times

armed soldier standing on each side of him. Bluebell was requested to sit down and the first question the man addressed to her was to ask in which language she would like the interview to be conducted. 'My own, if you please!' she answered. He pressed a buzzer on the desk and an elderly woman entered the room and sat down in another chair. Bluebell recalled that she looked extremely nervous and frightened. She was to be the interpreter for what followed. The interrogation began. 'We should like to know where your husband is.' The statement was translated from German into English. 'So would I!' retorted Bluebell.

The laborious process of translating everything that was said gave her time to think, and to be ready for the next question. Bluebell's excellent working knowledge of German, acquired during her years backstage at the Scala in Berlin, was of assistance to her in maintaining her control of a difficult situation.

En toutes Saisons venez à l'Alhambra !
Vous y verrez toujours un Spectacle des plus attrayant !

Above: wartime publicity for the Alhambra. Overleaf: the Chantilly Girls

Once or twice she responded too quickly. When she heard her interrogator say 'Ask if her husband would like to see his children again,' she interjected with 'Ask him if he would like to see his!' 'I think,' he said 'that you understand my language more than you will admit.' 'And I think,' replied Bluebell, 'that you understand mine more than *you* will admit.'

The interview lasted for more than an hour but, in spite of intensive questioning, the German was unable to force her to give herself away. Just how suspicious the Gestapo was is a matter for conjecture. In the case of any escaped prisoner it is likely that his wife will be an early target for questioning, and it is perhaps surprising that it had taken them several months to get around to her. There had been time enough for her to become pregnant again, and in spite of the evidence of Marcel's proximity visibly burgeoning within Bluebell, the interrogation officer did not make any comment on her condition, six months into the pregnancy, possibly out of some strange sense of delicacy. Bluebell had, in fact, prepared herself for such a reference, and was going to suggest that one did not examine a girl's morals too closely in wartime.

Finally, she was told that she could go. She was warned that she could shortly expect a home visit from the Gestapo. She raced back to the Rue Blanche, and carefully combed the flat for every vestige of evidence that would betray Marcel's existence, most of it in the form of socks and shirts she had been laundering, and found a secure hiding place. The anticipated visit never happened — either she had passed her examination so well that she was believed, or, as is more likely, the Gestapo had fatter fish to fry.

For the second time she had defeated a Nazi inquisition. She ascribes her ability to be able to tell outrageous lies without giving herself away through nervousness or an accelerated pulse, to a particular look that she has. 'I've never been shifty-eyed, I always looked them full in the face.' The skill she had developed in telling convincing stories had now been used to fool the ultimate professionals in detection techniques, the Gestapo itself.

On 22nd October 1943 Bluebell gave birth to her third child. This time it was a daughter. She was given the names Florence Kelly Marie Paule. Marcel, for obvious reasons, was unable to see the baby girl, but listened eagerly to the descriptions relayed to him. Patrick and Francis, who was by now a lively two-year-old, contemplated their new sister with fraternal pride.

Bluebell had only once broken her strict rule to keep the children away from the Rue Bertholet. On one particular occasion she had taken her two sons there to see their father, having carefully explained that the fact that he was there was a special secret to be divulged to no one. It is hard to curb childish excitement and, shortly after the visit, as they were making their way back home, they met Frederic Apcar, the man in Vaucresson who had been supplying her with extra food. 'We've just been to see pa—,' said Patrick, suddenly silenced by Bluebell clamping a hand over his mouth. Realizing that she was placing too high a burden on very young children, and that they could easily give the game away to the wrong person, she never repeated the experience.

Fear of detection was an ever-present hazard of daily life. Informers were everywhere, and hundreds of thousands of Frenchmen were betrayed by their compatriots for the sake of a modest reward. During a lull in her time at the Chantilly Bluebell was staging a modest show at the Théâtre des Optimistes. During a rehearsal she was called from the auditorium to face two plain clothes French policemen. 'We've had a report that you are an English Jewess,' said one of them. 'You are to come with us.'

Bluebell stood her ground. 'I'm not English — I'm Irish. And I'm not Jewish. I'm a Catholic, like you.' She produced her papers, including the letter that had enabled her to be released from Besançon, and made them read every detail. They were satisfied. 'We are sorry we have troubled you. But you see, we have to follow up every call we get, and this is what had been said about you!'

Bluebell never found out who had been responsible for giving the police false information about her, but since the consequences, had she been unable to prove its falsehood, would have been deportation and death, she concluded that it must have been someone who held a very strong grudge against her.

Christmas 1943 and the New Year passed with a feeling of optimism in the air. The Germans were now suffering serious military reverses. The Allies were fighting their way through Italy and in the east the Russians, after epic sieges such as those of Stalingrad and Leningrad, were now advancing inexorably. There was a feeling that the Second Front must

come any day, probably by the spring of 1944, and that the Third Reich would collapse. The Resistance became ever bolder, and factories, warehouses and railways were frequently sabotaged. There were also many air raids on the industrial sections of Paris, with the Renault plant at Boulogne-Billancourt, where tanks were in production, a particular target. When an air-raid warning occurred Paulette would gather up the children and take them down into the nearest Métro station, Pigalle, where they would wait on the dusty platforms with hundreds of other shelterers. Whereas in London the authorities had equipped deep Tube stations with bunk beds and other facilities enabling large numbers of people to avoid the bombs, no similar initiative was shown in Paris, and the population was required to fend for itself. The number of French civilians killed in Allied air raids was woefully large, but it was a reflection on the indifference of the ruling bodies to the plight of the people.

In April 1944, during a heavy raid, the Sacré Coeur at Montmartre was damaged, and Marshal Pétain made his only visit to Paris during the Occupation to inspect the damage. But although the raids were often very heavy it was rare for a landmark or historic building to be affected, the bombs generally being aimed at the suburbs. The geography of Paris assisted in the saving of the city, since almost all of the industrial plants were located on the outside of the *Boulevards Extérieurs*, the continuous ring road that encircled the compact inner city.

Occasionally the bombers swept in low enough for their markings to be plainly visible from the ground. Bluebell recalls seeing an American aircraft gradually descending, having been hit by a ground battery, a plume of thick black smoke streaming from a stricken engine. The crew, meanwhile, had baled out, and as they drifted slowly down to earth, helplessly dangling beneath their parachute canopies, she and scores of other people were horrified to see a Focke-Wulfe 190, a fast and manoeuvrable Luftwaffe fighter, repeatedly close in on the defenceless men, strafing them with its machine guns. It is unlikely that they survived.

The best news came early in June. It was impossible for the German propaganda machine to conceal from the people of Paris the information that a massive Allied landing had taken place on the shores of Normandy on the morning of the 6th. Its strategic importance was played down, however. It was, alleged the Germans, just a *divertissement*. The main event would come later, probably in the Pas de Calais area, and there was enough Panzer might in position there to hurl the invaders back into the sea. But the people of Paris went to bed that night knowing that American, Canadian, British and many of their own forces were on French soil, at the beginning of the fight to free them from the years of Nazi occupation. It was time for exhilaration, hope and rejoicing. But meanwhile, as long as the Germans remained amongst them, life would continue to be hard.

10   Resistance

MARCEL, TUCKED AWAY in his hideout in the Rue Bertholet, was becoming impatient. For well over two years he had been in hiding, unable to leave his quarters. He was reasonably comfortable — he had a shower and toilet facilities, as well as a tiny kitchen and larder. He relied on the concierge, not only to head off unwelcome strangers, but to see that his sanctuary remained hidden from the attention of snoopers. There were also the tiny details of normal life that had to be attended to, such as how the electricity and gas bills were to be paid, and these and other problems the concierge took under her wing, freeing him from some of the material headaches associated with his concealment. Mercifully, there were no serious structural matters needing the assistance of builders and plumbers, in spite of the severe shaking the building received during air raids. By remaining out of sight, and not allowing any lights to be seen at night through the heavy blackout blinds, he had been able to maintain a state of invisibility. But Marcel's position was scarcely unique. Throughout the city many thousands of fugitives wanted by the Germans were lying low, relying on friends and associates to keep them out of the hands of the enemy.

Bluebell made frequent visits to the Rue Bertholet on her bicycle, often with Marcel's washed laundry concealed in the basket slung between the handlebars, and she always made a point of giving the concierge around sixty francs a week to buy food and for making Marcel comfortable. She had to be careful when she called. It was advisable not to set up a routine, since regularity would be noticed and could give rise to eventual suspicion. But Bluebell was an active person, every day to be found pedalling along the Paris streets somewhere. Anyone attempting to follow her would soon have lost interest. In spite of her earlier brushes with the Gestapo she was certain that no one suspected that she was in regular contact with her husband, who, as an escapee, was automatically an enemy of the Reich, and liable to be shot instantly if found. But she remained on guard, constantly.

There had been two or three occasions when Marcel, desperate for a breath of freedom, had actually descended the stairs and gone out into the streets. Such an act of bravado was immensely dangerous, as Gestapo and SD men were everywhere, usually in plain clothes. It was always better to trust no one unless they were known intimately. He also had access to a telephone and had devised with Bluebell a way of sending coded messages to her, since open conversation, even on the automatic dial system, was liable to be monitored, particularly if, as in her case, there had already been an investigation by the Gestapo. A whole bureau had been established by the Germans to tap telephones in the hope of catching members of the Resistance, but its methods were so obvious that it was scarcely taken seriously.

Marcel's friend, Guy, also kept an eye on him, and would inform him on the current progress of the war. The news of the Allied progress in Normandy was encouraging, but conditions in Paris itself were visibly deteriorating at a rapid rate.

The most difficult days of the German occupation of Paris were the closing ones, and they were now at hand. After D-Day, the 6th June, it was clear that the Allies, having launched the biggest amphibious assault in history, had succeeded in establishing a foothold on Europe. Their Intelligence had brilliantly deceived the Germans, having laid false trails for many months. Rommel, expecting an attack in the Pas de Calais, had even been away in Germany on holiday as the landings took place, and the Führer reacted slowly, half believing that he was the victim of a monumental counter-bluff. Nevertheless, the Germans who defended the region fought bravely and determinedly, and in the days that followed D-Day inflicted far heavier casualties in the fields and villages of the Norman countryside than they had on the beaches. The major strategic objectives of Caen and Cherbourg were not to be a pushover — indeed, they would take many weeks to reach. Meanwhile the Wehrmacht took advantage of the Normandy *bocage*, the high hedgerows thick enough to conceal machine-gun posts and even the dreaded 88mm gun, which could penetrate the armour of a Sherman tank as though it were a paper bag. The Allies found that their

Bluebell on her wartime transport

tanks were slower, flimsier and more lightly armed than the Panzers, and only sheer weight of numbers eventually overwhelmed the German opposition.

In Paris food grew ever more scarce, and electricity supplies were so depleted that for the major part of the day the current was completely cut off. The warm spring and summer months eased the pressing problem of heating buildings and apartments, but cooking was still difficult, and various kinds of ingenious stoves were tried using alternative fuels such as scraps of newspaper, itself a commodity that became in short supply. Two out of three Parisians used bicycles to get around the city. Those people who had been given permission to run their own cars found that the privilege was an empty one since there was no petrol available. The *gazogène*, a wood or charcoal converter, was brought into use in the occupation years, and this huge and unsightly contraption would be bolted on to the rear of a vehicle, offering a bumpy, erratic ride with frequent back-firing. But even the fuel for *gazogènes* was now virtually unobtainable.

Public transport became ever more erratic. Some of the famous, if battered, green-and-cream buses, with their open rear platforms, ran with huge balloons affixed to their roofs which were filled with town gas to be used for propulsion. Others had *gazogènes* fitted immediately behind the driver. The Métro was unable, in the face of fuel shortages, to maintain its regular schedule. Many stations, and sometimes entire lines, were closed, and the platforms at the more important points of the system were frequently overcrowded to the point of danger as frustrated travellers awaited trains that never seemed to arrive.

The German occupying forces had become less impressed with the problems of running one of Europe's great cities, and more with those of saving their own skins. It was growing more apparent that when liberation came the Communists would attempt to provoke a civil insurrection in order that they could seize power. General de Gaulle, now acknowledged by Roosevelt, Churchill and the Allied Supreme Commander, General Dwight Eisenhower, as the French leader, stepped up his stirring broadcasts to the FFI, the *Forces Françaises de l'Intérieur*, or Free French, and used his considerable political skill to weld a coalition of the various political factions. Aware that he was to face formidable opposition from the Communists, he carefully laid his plans for the recovery of Paris. As more and more towns of northern France were liberated he ensured that Gaullist officials took charge of the new administrations, with the intention of heading off attempts by the Communists to seize control, while in Paris he infiltrated their organization with his own agents. It had been estimated that some 25,000 Communist guerrillas would take up arms in Paris, and de Gaulle regarded them as every bit as dangerous as the German garrison: one of the assumptions made by the advancing Allies which later proved to be exaggerated. The city, nevertheless, in the summer months of 1944, was in for a bumpy ride.

June became July, and the Allies came out of the *bocage*. Cherbourg had been entered on 27th June, opening up a major port and supply route which would ease the burden placed on the ingenious pontoon 'Mulberry' harbours. Caen was taken on 9th July, the ancient cathedral city reduced to a pitiful heap of rubble. On 17th July Rommel was badly injured after the RAF had strafed his car as it was moving along a country road, and he was pushed out of the war, replaced by Kluge, who had achieved distinction on the eastern front. Kluge was later to kill himself as defeat became certain.

And now the Resistance was beginning to emerge into the open. One of the miscalculations of the Allies was an underestimation of just how important the Resistance would be in the liberation of France. In the northwest, after the Cotentin peninsular had been recaptured, the advance through into Brittany had been relatively easy, with astonished troops finding that even in sizeable towns the Germans had already surrendered to the French themselves.

On 20th July came the sensational news that Hitler had been injured by a bomb which had exploded in his headquarters in Germany. Only by the merest fluke had he not been killed. Many of the conspirators were unaware of the failure of the plot, and swung into action a pre-arranged plan to wrest control from the Nazis, only to expose themselves and be arrested, and then to face humiliating trials and sadistic executions. Rommel, although not actively involved in the conspiracy, knew about it, and at Stuttgart, recovering from his head wounds, was invited by the Gestapo to take poison, thus enabling the Nazis to stage an elaborate state funeral as the empty and ironic homage to a great war hero.

In Paris there were several important figures in the plot who inadvertently gave themselves away, including General Heinrich von Stulpnagel, the military commander of the city. He attempted suicide, succeeded only in wounding himself, and was later tortured to death. Hitler, in a fit of manic revenge, decided that Paris must be destroyed, and appointed General Dietrich von Choltitz, renowned for his skill in laying waste such cities as Rotterdam and Sebastopol, to carry out the task.

The new military commander had realized even before he took up his post in Paris that the Führer had degenerated into an obviously raving madman, and that what he was contemplating would be one of the most monstrous crimes against civilization. Paris had to burn, Hitler had ordered — every building, every work of art, every priceless treasure. The population would be left to flee or die either in the flames or from the plagues and diseases that would ravage the ruins. To look upon the green trees in the Tuileries and the magnificent façade of the Palais du Louvre in the summer sunshine was enough to convince Choltitz that the orders he had been given were irrational to the point of insanity. As a loyal soldier he was obliged, however, to obey the orders of his commander, who might in the face of disobedience exact a terrible revenge on the Choltitz family inside Germany. It was a monumental dilemma.

Meanwhile the Allies were pressing nearer to the city. Several times a day aircraft bearing the white star of the new conquerors would sweep low making reconnaissance runs and unnerving the German defenders. At Falaise the Germans had held a wedge between the British and American armies, but in spite of fierce resistance they were eventually overwhelmed. The push to the Seine was now on in earnest.

On 15th August American forces had landed in the South of France and met little opposition. Although the Germans did not regard the loss of the French Riviera as a serious strategic blow the news further increased the new nationalist fervour that was awakening. In Paris the police staged a strike. There was an element of self-protection in the action, for they were mindful that, as the servants of the German occupiers, they had carried out much of their messy business in rounding up enemies of the Reich, and they would thus be regarded as collaborators after the liberation, and expect to face unpleasant reckonings. The representatives of the Resistance within the police gave notice that anyone disobeying the strike call would be regarded as a traitor and dealt with accordingly.

Aux barricades! A street near the Hôtel de Ville on 20th August 1944

The city was now in the depths of a terrible crisis. Stocks of food and fuel were dwindling to danger levels and not being replenished. There were no coal supplies left to feed the power stations, and thus no electricity. The last trainload of prisoners to be deported from France left Paris on the 15th. Choltitz now gave the order that remaining detainees would be released, both those in police custody and the thousands who were in the hands of the Germans.

Eisenhower had not wanted to liberate Paris, preferring to bypass it and strike at Germany itself, thus bringing the war to a conclusion. He had argued that if Paris was left under a temporary German control the responsibility for the population would not dog the Allied footsteps. The petrol alone needed each day to maintain the essential food supplies for the city's population would in itself be enough to move an entire army corps twenty-five miles. De Gaulle, on the other hand, vigorously argued that Paris must be freed or else insurrection would take place and then Communist rule would prevail.

Events were, in any case, running ahead of the argument. The Métro workers followed the example of the police and stopped working. The Resistance became bolder and began to appear openly. The Germans carried on with their packing, ready to move out. By the 17th the exodus was in full spate. The last train left the concentration camp at Drancy, bearing its

A beaten-up collaborator is removed by the police

commandant and his staff. It was the seventy-eighth trainload of the Occupation, and of the eighty thousand Jews deported only a few hundred survived. More than a quarter of the Jewish population of Paris was murdered by the Nazis. When the last train had gone the gates were left open behind it, and the remaining prisoners abandoned to fend for themselves.

Marcel's car, in storage in the garage off the Rue Blanche, was found by the Germans, who noted that the tyres were in good condition. Rubber was one of the great wartime shortages, and a good set of tyres a considerable prize. Later that day, Bluebell received a call from the garage owner telling her that German soldiers had stripped off the tyres and also taken the expensive car radio. She went down to see what damage had been inflicted on the vehicle. The proprietor, responding to her indignation, suggested that she should seek compensation from the German authorities, who, surprisingly, in the past had met small claims of this sort, and gave her a certificate recording the losses.

The following morning Bluebell set out on her bicycle to the relevant office off the Champs-Elysées. Although she arrived at 9 a.m. there was already in front of her a queue of around thirty people, all men, most of them like her clutching scraps of paper in their hands. Most of the clerks were engaged in emptying filing cabinets, removing and destroying papers, and giving less than full attention to the French civilians. But after a wait of nearly half-an-hour a German major pulled her out of the line and invited her into his office. He enquired what her problem was, and when Bluebell answered in English continued the conversation in that language. She explained what had happened and that she wanted compensation. The German officer at first suggested that she should approach the French, but Bluebell insisted that as the problem had been caused by the Germans it was they who should be dealing with it.

Although he retained his politeness he clearly felt that he was up against a determined woman who was likely to prove an intolerable nuisance unless some solution was found. He looked at the garage docket and then asked to see the certificate of ownership for the car. Bluebell realized that she had left it at home. She was told that if she went back to get it and came in again her claim would be met in full. He told her emphatically that she would have to be back by eleven o'clock as they were in the process of leaving, and there would be no one left to help her after that time.

Bluebell, set on getting the Germans to pay, hastily left the building and remounted her bicycle. The traffic on the Champs Elysées consisted almost entirely of bicycles, but as she approached the Place de la Concorde she saw three buses lined up and a number of young people climbing aboard. They were, she assumed, being rounded up by the Germans. Then as she entered the broad expanse of the Place itself she heard a series of sharp popping noises, and took it that the sounds were coming from a charcoal converter on a vehicle. Then suddenly she realized that all the other people who had been riding on bicycles had disappeared, having fled to the sides of the square. She was on her own in the middle of an empty expanse of roadway and bullets were flying over her head.

What was happening was that the Resistance, dug in around the foot of the Pont de la Concorde on the river bank, were engaged in a fierce gun battle with the Germans, who were holed up in the Naval Ministry on the north-east corner of the Place de la Concorde. Bluebell, suddenly aware of what was happening, fell off her bicycle and lay frozen with one leg still in the air, too terrified even to move it down. Eventually she gingerly lowered the upraised limb from its inelegant position, but still lay there with the bicycle firmly lodged between her legs. She could see German machine gunners on the roof of the naval building, and could actually discern the path of the bullets as they sped through the air over her head. For half-an-hour she remained motionless, praying that some marksman would not decide to take a shot at her. And then, as though on a signal, the firing stopped. The battle was over. There was a stirring at the sides of the Place as people began to move about again. Bluebell remained where she was. Then she saw a German soldier carrying a machine gun approaching her. She could see that he was very young, probably no more than eighteen, and looked somewhat frightened. As he came up to her, probably to check whether she

French Resistance members and Americans rout out a German sniper's nest

was unharmed by the firing, Bluebell yelled at him in English: 'Go away! You can bloody well hop it!' He was so startled that he hastily backed off, possibly wondering what a mad Englishwoman was doing in the middle of the Place de la Concorde, and if she represented some advance force of British undercover troops.

Bluebell then got up and started to walk away, but decided after going a few yards that it was crazy to leave her bicycle where it was, so she went back and retrieved it, and then slowly she wheeled it to a tobacconist's shop in the Rue Royale which was run by a friend. When she crossed the threshold there she keeled over in a dead faint. It took her several minutes to come round, and when she did so she found the shopkeeper bending over her solicitously. Naturally, as the Place de la Concorde was only a short distance away, he had heard the shooting and had kept the shop boarded up. He was dumbfounded when he heard Bluebell's account of events, and when she had fully recovered he personally helped to see her, with her bicycle, back to the Rue Blanche.

The battle in the Place de la Concorde was not an isolated incident.

COGNAC FURLAUD

Life after liberation—an appeal to the Allies

Outbreaks of fighting were taking place all over the city, as more members of the Resistance took up arms. Choltitz was approached by the Swedish Consul General, Raoul Nordling, who proposed a truce, or cease fire, to enable normal life to resume, an idea that proved attractive to the German, as he badly needed to redeploy his pinned-down troops so that they could defend the city against the Allied armies.

Meanwhile, Hitler was reinforcing his insane demands that Choltitz destroy the city, and ordered that all the Seine bridges be blown up, even though to do so would be to hamper the Germans' own troop movements. Choltitz now made his most momentous decision. Rather than be remembered in history as the man who had carried out the destruction of Paris, he decided that the city should not be harmed. It was better that a negotiated truce be arranged with the Resistance to allow the Germans to move out in an orderly fashion. Unfortunately, the Communists felt that they had been left out of the discussions, and quickly saw to it that the truce became unworkable. Molotov cocktails were hurled at German troop carriers, snipers mowed down German soldiers from the rooftops. There was nothing that the Gaullists could do to bring the guerrilla fighting to a standstill.

Both Hitler and Eisenhower were apprehensive at the news of the unrest on the streets. Hitler repeated his orders for Choltitz to blow up the city. The fact that most of the troops under his command were engaged in coping with the street fighting was the excuse Choltitz proffered to General Jodl, Hitler's chief of staff. Eisenhower knew that he would have to face de Gaulle, who would demand the diversion of Allied resources to effect the liberation of Paris, and suspected that the Germans had reinforced the defences and the whole thing could be a monumental trap. De Gaulle, harping on the threat of a Communist takeover following civil insurrection, stormed and blustered until he secured the Allied High Command's decision to liberate the city. He insisted that Paris must be retaken by the French themselves as an expression of national pride which, de Gaulle recognized, would have to be carefully nurtured after the débâcle of 1940.

It was eventually agreed by a weary Eisenhower that the French 2nd Armoured Division, under the command of Major General Jacques Leclerc, should perform the historic task. Leclerc's division, ironically composed mainly of soldiers from the French colonies — Indochina, Chad, Morocco, Tunisia, Senegal — most of whom had never set foot in France before although they were officially French nationals, was positioned about a hundred miles west of Paris. Meanwhile, many of its citizens, not for the first time in its long, and sometimes turbulent saga, went to the barricades. There was now a full-blown general strike, and in the absence of a gendarmerie to halt it, paving stones were uprooted, trees felled, vehicles overturned to block streets and trap the Boche. Resistance newspapers were openly hawked on the streets, rallying the people into action. Key buildings were seized and turned into strongholds. Swastika flags were torn down and the French Tricolour unfurled in their place. The FFI wore armbands with the Cross of Lorraine symbol on them for identification — and for easy disposal if they found themselves falling into German hands.

Two deputations somehow got through the perimeter lines and met up with the Allies in the west. Two anti-Communist Resistance members gave graphic accounts of events to General Patton himself, who was at first unimpressed, but agreed to pass them on to General Bradley's headquarters, where a meeting with Leclerc was imminent. Nordling, meanwhile, had secured permission from Choltitz to make an attempt to see de Gaulle. Just before he was due to leave he had a heart attack, and the deputation was led instead by his brother. But by the time they reached the Allied command, Leclerc's advance had already begun.

The date was 23rd August. At first his armoured division encountered more resistance from the unseasonal rains which lashed the narrow country roads, making progress hazardous, than from opposing German forces. To supplement Leclerc's forces Bradley had ordered part of the American 4th Infantry Division to approach from the south. There was great urgency to get there to ease the peril in which the population was placed, but a new hazard impeded progress. At every town and village encountered along the route the whole population would turn out, blocking the road, insisting on garlanding the troops, embracing them and showering them with gifts. It was hard to dampen the joy of these people by spurning their welcome, but it was necessary to do so.

Choltitz, although anxious to spare Paris from destruction, was still prepared to make a fight of it, on the outskirts at least, and had been busily deploying his Panzers to head off Leclerc. He was first and foremost a soldier, and his sense of military honour demanded that he defend his command to the best of his abilities. The night of the 24th was spent by Leclerc's troops in bivouac at Rambouillet, and de Gaulle arrived to install himself in the great château there, which was only thirty miles from the centre of Paris.

The following day Leclerc split his division into three columns and prepared to assault the perimeter defences of the city. There was some confusion at Bradley's headquarters because he had gone out of radio contact, and some unkind voices were suggesting that his troops had succumbed to the alcoholic hospitality lavished on them by the liberated people en route. It was an unjust slur, for Leclerc now faced some very heavy fighting against the German 88s and their Tiger tanks. The French in their American-built Shermans with their thin armour-plating were often outclassed, and casualties were heavy. By the evening there was still another ten miles to go. Then a tank captain reported to Leclerc that he had found an unguarded gap in the German defences. Leclerc ordered him to go through and enter the city, in order to make a gesture that would boost the morale of the people.

Just before 9.30 that evening three Shermans in the captain's detachment, and six half-tracks bearing the Allied white star, entered inner Paris at the Porte de Gentilly, made their way to the Place d'Italie and from there along the Boulevard de l'Hôpital and across the Seine at the Pont d'Austerlitz, to turn westwards along the Right Bank. They entered the Place de l'Hôtel de Ville, in the historic centre of Paris, to the delight of the people watching, and pulled up in front of the old city hall. It was still daylight, with the shadows lengthening in the evening sunshine. Their arrival was a signal for the bells of Notre-Dame, silent for four years, to ring out across the city. Their ecstatic peals were then joined by the bells of many of the other churches. Their message to the people of Paris was clear: the day they had waited for since 1940 was at hand.

In Bluebell's apartment in the Rue Blanche the telephone rang. She picked it up. It was Marcel. 'I'm coming home,' he said.

11   Liberation

MARCEL MADE HIS WAY openly across the river and up to the Rue Blanche to receive the warmest of greetings from a daughter he had never seen before, and who had now become a lively walker and talker aged one-and-a-quarter, as well as his two sons who had not been with him for two years. For the children his homecoming was the most exciting event of the liberation period, and the little apartment was filled with the most innocent and unaffected joy. For Marcel the ever-present fear of denunciation under which he had existed during his years in hiding was at last thrown aside, a condition that would take him some few days to appreciate. For Bluebell there was a feeling of quiet satisfaction that at last, as she had always predicted, the Germans were being sent packing and Paris could get back to normal.

On the morning of 25th August, the bulk of Leclerc's 2nd Armoured Division now rolled into the central part of the city, closely followed by many units of the American 4th Infantry Division. The Parisians poured on to the streets, ecstatic with joy, overwhelming the soldiers with their jubilation. Long-hidden national flags were hung from almost every window, while reserve stocks of champagne, hidden away throughout the occupation, were brought out and donated to the conquerors. Girls hugged and kissed them, and the older people cried '*Merci, merci*', tears running down their faces.

There were still more than 20,000 Germans in the city, some of whom were determined to fight to the last. Even as the crowds surged through the streets singing the Marseillaise and waving their Tricolours, fighting was still going on. Rooftop snipers were particularly dangerous, and there were many casualties among civilians as well as the Allied forces, some tragically the result of lapses in caution due to the euphoria wrought by alcohol.

Marcel and Bluebell were back together in the Rue Blanche for the first time since 1941, but even now it was not all over. They watched with horror from their window some last-ditch Germans on the roof of the restaurant across the street shoot at people on the other side of the Place Blanche, outside the Moulin Rouge, with resulting casualties. Armed men of the FFI eventually managed to flush them out.

The morning was a hectic one. Jeeps with white flags forced their way through the streets, bearing officers with orders to attempt to negotiate truce terms with some of the isolated pockets of Germans. They mingled with carloads of Resistance men, now proudly displaying their membership with makeshift banners. The American war correspondent Ernest Hemingway had apparently reached the Ritz Hotel in the Place Vendôme and headed straight for the bar, where he ordered seventy-three dry martinis for himself and for the lucky people with him. Leclerc made his way slowly from the Gare Montparnasse, where he had established his new headquarters, to the Prefecture, to attend a victory luncheon hurriedly organized by members of the Resistance. At the same time, much heavy fighting had been going on around the Hotel Meurice, the headquarters of Choltitz. At 2.30 p.m. word was brought to Leclerc while he was still at the lunch. The German commander had at last been captured, and was waiting with a guard of American GIs in the next room. Choltitz had been brought there through crowds of hissing, spitting Parisians, then unaware of his efforts to spare them from the consequences of Hitler's insane plan of destruction, even though he had been obliged to wire up some of the major landmarks with high explosives which he had prayed would never be triggered. Leclerc heard the interesting news, nodded and excused himself from the table. His ensuing dealings with Choltitz were brisk and formal. By 3 p.m. the document of surrender had been signed, and Paris had officially fallen, not to the Allies, but to the French, another wish of de Gaulle's that Leclerc had schemed to fulfil.

De Gaulle himself arrived in Paris an hour later, driving through the streets in an open civilian limousine, acknowledging the cheers of the crowds with his characteristically stiff-armed wave, and showing total indifference to the occasional sounds of gunfire from the few remaining pockets of German resistance, even though his tall, craggy and unmistakeable figure was a sitting target for a sniper. De Gaulle had

De Gaulle, triumphant on 26th August 1944

mentally rehearsed this day for four years, and was determined not to deviate from the scenario he had mentally worked out.

The joy continued through the evening. There was dancing in the streets as darkness fell, and for once blackout regulations went by the board. There had not been a day like it in anyone's lifetime.

The following day de Gaulle had arranged for a very special piece of theatre for the people of Paris. There was to be a magnificent victory parade through the streets, which he would lead. It was, he hoped, going to be regarded as a Gallic display of political unity, and a way of asserting his brand of government over that of the Communists.

His first task was to inspect the lined-up tanks and half-tracks, together with their crews, who in spite of having recently been in battle made themselves as spruce and tidy as possible. At the Arc de Triomphe he briefly conferred with the leader of the Resistance, Georges Bidault, as they contemplated the eternal flame, and then with Leclerc and many eminent civilians he walked on foot down the Champs-Elysées, acknowledging the tumultuous acclaim of the people, many of whom had been gathering there from 7 a.m. onwards to be certain of a place at such an historic occasion. There were crowds everywhere in Paris that day, and the Place de l'Opéra was packed with people, even though it was not on the processional route.

As the marching column reached the Place de la Concorde, the scene of Bluebell's adventure a few days earlier, shots again rang out, and many thousands of people simultaneously ducked for cover. De Gaulle maintained a cool dignity, and boarded an open car to continue his progress to the Hôtel de Ville. There was more shooting in that area, too, this time from machine guns hidden in buildings around the Place de l'Hôtel de Ville, and there was near panic as the crowds scrambled to get out of range. It did not deter de Gaulle, who, after a brief halt, moved on to Notre-Dame, the great cathedral of Paris, where there was yet more shooting as he alighted from his car, with men of the FFI on the street returning the Germans' fire. Gunfire was even exchanged within the cathedral itself. De Gaulle appeared to be superbly indifferent to the physical danger and walked sedately down the aisle to his place at the front of the congregation without so much as a hint of fear crossing his face. The service was brief, but to the point — a Te Deum for deliverance, followed by more bell-ringing — and when de Gaulle left, once again to endure the barrage of gun fire outside, he preserved his mien so well that at that moment he could have taken possession of the whole of France. He was determined to establish himself as a legend, and his apparent indestructibility would in due course be put to the test.

Bluebell and Marcel were among the crowds who had gone out to see the victory parade and to catch a glimpse of the General. Fortunately, they took up their position in the Champs-Elysées above the point where the trouble began. It was estimated that the liberation of Paris claimed the lives of more than a thousand of its citizens, most of them members of the FFI, in the various skirmishes that took place in the streets.

One of the most chilling discoveries made by the liberators was that on 25th August, the day of the German surrender, there had been only sufficient food and fuel supplies in the city to last one day further. General Eisenhower's view that the relief of Paris would divert the campaign effort proved to be totally accurate, but the needs of humanity had to be served. So Eisenhower was obliged to order an immediate airlift, and within a matter of hours a score of C-47 transports, the famous Douglas 'Dakota' aircraft, were ferrying in food, medical supplies and other basic needs at the rate of 500 tons a day. There can be no question that recovering Paris slowed the advance, and in all probability delayed the end of the war, for by December 1944 the going had become very tough, and the Germans impeded progress by launching their suicidal, but devastating Bastogne offensive in the Ardennes. A swift, untrammelled thrust by the Allies in the summer of 1944 into Germany would have spiked that initiative. It took the Germans an extraordinarily long time to lose the war, and ingenious technology was mustered to provide the last punches. London and south-east England suffered a constant bombardment during that summer from the V1 pilotless flying-bombs, which were launched from sites in north-east France and the Low Countries. When those sites were taken a new, more terrifying weapon was unleashed, the V2 rocket, the first such missile which could reach its target faster than the speed of sound, and was able to flatten perhaps a dozen buildings and damage hundreds more on impact. There were other V weapons in the pipeline, but there was insufficient time for them to be developed in adequate numbers, so they were never used. The Germans did, however, get the first operational jet fighter aircraft, the ME 262, into the air, where its speed outclassed anything in the air forces of the Allies, but it proved so difficult to fly that its usefulness was limited.

Three days after de Gaulle had made his famous walk on foot through the Paris streets, Eisenhower himself was present for an even more magnificent victory parade, with de Gaulle, Bradley and Leclerc among those on the saluting base, reviewing an entire division of the US Army, the 28th Infantry. It was an impressive show of strength, and de Gaulle reaped the political kudos as vehicle after vehicle rumbled down the Champs-Elysées. There was even a practical purpose in the deployment of so many fighting men. Once the processional route had been covered the long convoy, with its truckloads of soldiers in full battle order, stepped up its pace and sped off to reach the advancing Allied line as it spread eastwards across France.

There were thousands of German prisoners, all of whom had to be processed before being sent on to the camps. Many of them were put to work clearing up the debris in the streets. The French themselves gleefully uprooted all the German direction signs, and consigned them to impromptu bonfires. Within a matter of days it was as though the Germans had never been there — every swastika had been torn down, every Nazi poster

Les Swing Folies girls from Follies Cocktail

obliterated, and fresh paint was found to cover up signs painted directly on walls. The speed with which these operations were carried out was given the full backing of the authorities. De Gaulle, his anxieties for a civil insurrection fading, knew that the temper of the people would have to be defused, and restoring the face of the city was an obvious way to do it.

There was an ugly side to the liberation. Those who had collaborated with the Germans received a harsh come-uppance. In many cases they were shot out-of-hand, in others executed after the most perfunctory trials. The prison at Fresnes, the doors of which had only a week or two earlier been opened to allow the inmates to go free, was now filled with people who had been too friendly towards the Germans. The spirit of denunciation was as rampant as ever, but the sides had switched. It was also a time for the settling of old scores, and it is impossible to say how many of the thousands of French people executed — one estimate puts it as high as over a hundred thousand — were actually innocent, and merely victims of those who wanted them out of way in case their own misdeeds should be revealed.

The petty collaborators were beaten and spat upon by the crowds of vengeance-seekers who were not able to repress four years of pent-up rage. Some people were literally kicked and hacked to death at the hands of the mobs in scenes that resembled the Reign of Terror at the end of the eighteenth century. What happened in the days following the liberation was significant — as though there was taking place some apocalyptic purging of the guilt of France through further bloodshed, and if the estimate of those who died is correct it exceeded in number those who were sent from Paris to their deaths in the Nazi extermination camps.

The treatment for women who had fraternized with the enemy was straightforward and simple. Their heads were shaved to the skin. They were then forced to walk through the streets with much of their clothing torn off, their breasts exposed, and sometimes with slogans announcing their shame scrawled in lipstick across their torsos. The shorn head was a humiliating badge, and it was difficult for such women to be seen in public until the hair had grown back, for a concealing headscarf was immediately recognized for what it was. The prostitutes were the ones who suffered more than most as it became difficult for them to ply their trade without any hair.

Among those whose heads were shaven was the concierge of the building in which Marcel had been concealed, although there had been only a few grey locks for her to lose. Bluebell was surprised to receive a telephone call from the concierge's granddaughter telling her what had happened and explaining that the old woman was now in police custody. Bluebell was indignant and appalled at this apparent miscarriage of justice. She promised that she would do all she could to help, and went off to see the officer in charge of the police station in which the concierge was held. Bluebell explained patiently to the inspector how her husband had been cared for while he was in hiding, and that he had been treated with exemplary kindness by her. So powerfully did Bluebell testify on the woman's behalf that the police decided to release her, and she went back home. It was, however, not to be the end of the story.

Two hours later the granddaughter telephoned Bluebell again, this time in an even greater state of distress. For the second time Bluebell went to the police station. On this second occasion she found that for once she was required to do the listening. It seemed that the apparently sweet old lady, far from being an unjustly accused innocent, had been responsible for betraying several loyal Frenchmen who had spent time hiding in the rooms of her apartment building. In each instance where she had betrayed someone she had been paid a reward of fifty francs. Therein lay the reason why Marcel had been spared from denunciation. Bluebell had been paying her sixty francs a week, plus various gifts of scarce food such as eggs or condensed milk which she had bought from Frederic Apcar. A mere ten francs had therefore saved her husband's life. Bluebell was aghast, never having suspected that such disgraceful perfidy had reached out so closely to her, while Marcel, perhaps less astonished, accepted his good fortune. It was a reinforcement of the unofficial rule of the occupation years — that no one should be trusted. The woman was eventually tried for her crimes and given a long sentence which in view of her age she could never complete, for Bluebell heard not very long afterwards that she had died in prison.

For the first time since she had been held in Besançon Bluebell was able to communicate with Mary Murphy in Liverpool, and was relieved to learn that the bombing of the city had not affected her. Mary Murphy had only a scant idea of what had happened to Bluebell, but had faithfully prayed for the deliverance of her foster-daughter and her family. She was overjoyed a few days after the liberation of Paris to receive a brief message that they were all well, which was followed up with pages of detailed accounts of how life had been for the Leibovicis in the intervening four years. Bluebell promised her that as soon as the war ended and travel to the continent had again become possible she would bring her over to Paris.

Paris was free, but the war was decidedly not over. Some of the euphoric mood of liberation had washed over the armies, and the mistaken view that the Germans were already beaten caused efforts to slacken. The British commander of the land forces, General Montgomery, not only relinquished the job to Eisenhower, but became involved in a fierce dispute on strategy, arguing that a single thrust into Germany would be more effective than the broad front policy of his superior. Eisenhower, obliged to balance the conflicting desires of other commanders under his control, the most temperamental being General Patton, was forced to conduct the campaign politically as well as strategically, and even his optimism became dulled by September 1944 when Montgomery's daring plan to outflank the Germans by seizing the bridge at Arnhem came seriously unstuck.

Paris was once more the target of German air raids, and was even briefly under threat of the V1s until the launching sites that were within range were captured. The blackout was still necessary, but the oppressive curfew decreed by the Germans was removed. Within two months of liberation de Gaulle had reorganized the municipal authority, replacing the collaborators and nominees of Pétain with Gaullist members of the Resistance. Those members of the Resistance who had not been stood down joined the regular French army.

The Allies followed the Germans in looking on the city as a gigantic leave centre. For that reason the authorities had ordered that as soon as electricity supplies became more reliable places of entertainment should endeavour to get back to normal. For Bluebell and Marcel it meant that once again they could work in their respective fields without restriction. It was hard, however, for Marcel to forgive Paul Derval at the Folies Bergère for subscribing to the Nazi anti-Jewish line. In vain Derval endeavoured to explain that he had no choice — had he not done so the Germans would have taken over his theatre. He had been able to keep going sporadically during the occupation under his own steam, although the shows were shadows of the pre-war Folies. There would, of course, be many Wehrmacht uniforms in the audience but Derval did not fall into the trap that so many people in the entertainment world found themselves in, of directly performing to exclusively German audiences. Many of the great stars, including Chevalier and Mistinguett, faced post-war unpopularity on that account.

By October 1944 the Paris theatres, music halls and cabarets were back in business, which was booming. The Allied Committee on Welfare and Recreation became a theatre agency for the troops, offering free or low-priced tickets to such famous establishments as the Olympia and the Empire. The British organization responsible for amusing the forces, ENSA, took over the Marigny Theatre to put on stage plays that might have come straight from Shaftesbury Avenue. At 144 Champs-Elysées a Stage Door Canteen was opened up, a voluntarily run night club for the services, offering entertainment and dancing with partners on tap. The institution, modelled on those in Hollywood, New York and London, was barred to officers, catering only for other ranks in the British forces, or enlisted men as they were called in the American army.

Derval rushed to get a new show into rehearsal at the Folies Bergère even as the bells of liberation were pealing, and two months later opened *Follies-Cocktail*, for once breaking the rule that each title should consist of thirteen letters. Its director was still Maurice Hermite, with support from Michel Gyarmathy, who would go on to stage all the post-war shows. Bluebell agreed to return after her long absence, but was shocked at how run-down the backstage area of the famous theatre had become, but all the available and limited resources were put to making the show look as good as possible from the audience's point of view — the out-of-sight improvements having

The Moulin Rouge at the end of the war. Overleaf: A scene from Folies Cocktail

to wait until conditions generally had eased. She had to recruit her dancers from Paris as it was impossible to bring girls in from England while the war was still on, and she also felt that the severe rationing that was in force at that time would not make France very attractive for visitors. She had not realized that the British were enduring food shortages every bit as onerous, and were well-used to the harshness of wartime conditions.

Meanwhile, at the same time as she was recruiting her girls to appear in the new show at the Folies, Bluebell continued looking after a small troupe of dancers at the Chantilly, the little cabaret theatre in the Montmartre district, which continued to flourish under its new conditions, much as it had during the occupation years. There had been few German uniforms seen there; but now there were plenty of French and American soldiers seeking the place out. It was still a favourite haunt of black marketeers, for whom interesting new possibilities for business had been opened up by the American presence. Cigarettes, for instance, had virtually become a hard currency in their own right in the strained economic climate of the day, and the GIs seemed to have, through the PXs, or military shops, roughly equivalent to the British NAAFI, unlimited access to the cherished American brands such as Camel and Lucky Strike. Other sought-after commodities included candy, toiletries and the then fabulous nylon stockings, which sent Frenchwomen wild with excitement, many of them had been reduced to applying makeshift make-up, and drawing the black seam up the back of the leg with an eyebrow pencil. The racketeers were willing to pay good money for such merchandise, so the Chantilly, ostensibly a small cabaret with dancing and entertainment, was an unofficial trade centre. Even the occasional visits by patrols of 'snowballs', as the white-helmeted military policemen were called, could not put an end to such transactions.

The Christmas of 1944, the last of the war, and the first to be spent in a free Paris since 1939, was marred by events in Belgium, where the Allies, their supply lines now stretched to breaking point, faced a massive and bloody counter-attack by the Germans, who tried to break out through the Ardennes and make for Antwerp, cutting the Allied armies in two. The capture of Antwerp had been an empty victory in any case because the estuary through which the port was reached remained in German hands. The Americans now found that at a time when they had hoped that victory was in their pockets they were obliged to fight to the death a determined enemy totally unwilling to give in.

It was a vain last fling, and in January of 1945 the so-called Battle of the Bulge had petered out. In the east, meanwhile, the Russians continued their inexorable progress, so that Germany was caught in a tightening clamp, the pressure applied from both sides. As the final victory grew near the American president, Franklin D. Roosevelt, who had been noticeably tired and ill at the Yalta conference with Churchill and Stalin, died. The suicide of his hated adversary, Adolf Hitler, followed shortly afterwards, with the

Russians then taking Berlin and accepting the surrender of all German forces. Thus ended the war in Europe. On VE-Day, as 8th May was designated, the capitals of Europe, with the notable exception of Berlin, celebrated and gave thanks for peace.

In some respects in Paris it was a reprise of the scenes in the preceding August, but with nothing like the same exhilaration. The day passed and the people went back to the task of recovery. It was the age of the refugee and the displaced person, as those who had lost everything, including, in some cases, their countries, were called. The survivors of the Nazi prison camps came home, emaciated and bemused. In most cases they were lucky still to be alive, and would wear their tattooed concentration camp numbers as a private memorial to their fellow inmates who had died. It was also an age of depressing shortages, particularly of food and housing, and temporary camps, reminiscent in appearance to those lately vacated in Germany, had to be set up for the homeless.

The Leibovicis managed to get their Citroën back on to the road again, with refurbished wheels. By saving their petrol ration they were able to make the drive to Normandy to see what had happened to their little retreat there. Wisely, it had been registered in Bluebell's name, as any property belonging to Jews had been confiscated. Miraculously, Ireland's neutrality had been upheld. The house was undamaged, intact and untouched, and a few hours of heavy scrubbing restored it to its pristine appearance.

Bluebell was not happy with the conditions prevailing at the Folies Bergère. The theatre backstage was dirty and her girls were badly paid. After a number of flare-ups Bluebell decided that she could no longer go on with it. The spell had in any case been broken at the start of the war, and the treatment she and Marcel had received still rankled. During the second season there after its post-liberation reopening she asked to be released from her contract, even though it was going to represent a considerable drop in her income. Marcel had only briefly returned to the Folies after the liberation, working as the pianist in the orchestra, a post he regarded as something of a stopgap, for shortly afterwards he left with a better offer, to form his own orchestra at the Pigalle.

Bluebell was not out of work for very long. She was asked to help with a show at Les Ambassadeurs, a theatre-restaurant in the Avenue Gabriel, which runs parallel to the lower section of the Champs-Elysées, close to the Place de la Concorde. One night after the show she went with her husband and two friends to see the Lido, which had been reopened by a new management in premises directly on the Champs-Elysées. Her visit was made largely out of curiosity to see what had been done to the place. While she was in the bar someone approached her and said that M. Guérin would welcome having a quick word with her. At that time she had no idea who he was, but decided to find out. He turned out to be the manager. He had one question for her. 'Would you be interested in doing the next show here?'

12   A New Beginning

IT WAS THE SUMMER of 1946, the first summer of peace. Paris was still full of uniforms, and military vehicles cruised the avenues and boulevards, often outnumbering civilian cars, but the old spirit of the city was slowly reviving as memories of recent years began to recede. It was the year of the Nuremburg trials, when not only the surviving leaders of the Nazi party faced an Allied court to answer for their war crimes, but hundreds of smaller fry also received condign punishment. In France the leaders of Vichy were tried and sentenced — Pétain to life imprisonment, Laval to execution — as France purged the bitter aftertaste of war. The countries of Eastern Europe became satellites of Soviet Russia, and Germany was divided between four powers — the United States, Britain, France and Russia — with Berlin, an enclave within the Russian zone, further divided into four sectors.

There were still acute food shortages throughout most of Europe, and rationing remained in force. In Britain the people were astonished that post-war rationing was even more stringent than at the height of the war, and in 1946 even bread could only be obtained on coupons, with potatoes being added in the following year. Nevertheless, some signs that peacetime had arrived were apparent, one of them being the relaxation of restrictions

159

The Leibovicis' country home in Normandy

affecting foreign travel. It was once again possible to journey across the English Channel without special permits, and the civilian ferries, many of which had performed sterling service in wartime, some even taking part in the 1940 Dunkirk evacuation, started up once more, carrying innocent cargoes of holidaymakers and schoolchildren visiting the continent for the first time. The biggest hindrances imposed, apart from the general shortage of accommodation available in most European cities, stemmed from the exchange control regulations which severely limited the amount of currency that could be taken out of the country. It was best to have friends and relations abroad who could provide bed and board during the stay.

Bluebell had long promised Mary Murphy that she was going to bring her to France. Before the war the pace of life had been such that there had never been a chance, and Aunt Mary had never been particularly enthusiastic about making the trip. The long war years had changed her attitude, and now she relished the prospect. Bluebell sent her a ticket that was to take her from Lime Street station in Liverpool, down to London, on to Folkestone and then across the channel to Boulogne and a French train which a couple of hours later pulled into the Gare du Nord in the heart of Paris. Bluebell met her at the barrier, Mary Murphy a tiny, frail, grey figure, clearly in awe of the great city in which she now found herself. They made slow progress in a taxi to the Rue Blanche. The streets were filled with people, all in a joyful mood. In some places they were even dancing on the cobblestones to impromptu melodies squeezed out on accordions, like extras in an old Chevalier movie. Mary Murphy had never seen anything like it in her life. Finally the taxi pulled up at the street door of the Leibovicis' apartment. 'I do like Paris!' the old lady sighed. 'To be dancing in the streets like this is wonderful — is it like this every night?' Bluebell was unable to confirm to her that it was — for her first visit to France unwittingly had coincided with 14th July, '*le quartorze juillet*', the most important of France's national holidays.

Now there were a husband and three children to meet the woman who had raised Bluebell from babyhood. They had heard much about her for so many years, but now came the chance to see her for the first time. The apartment was smaller than ever, and Bluebell realized that their days in the Rue Blanche were now numbered, as a much larger place was needed. They had, however, sold off their country home, and bought a larger, grander place with two or three acres of lush pasture surrounding it, also in Normandy, not far from Anet. It was there that Mary Murphy spent most of her six-week stay, with the children, the serenity of the countryside giving her a much-needed rest. She insisted, however, in attending early-morning Mass come what may, and would be up and out at 7 a.m., although the service was conducted in a language she could not understand and even the church Latin pronunciation was scarcely recognizable to her.

Eventually Mary Murphy decided that she could stay no longer, as she was missing her West Derby home. There were certain creature comforts denied her in France, a proper cup of tea, for example, and friendly chats with her neighbours. In Normandy few people could speak English, and she felt that she was too old to learn French. So she packed her suitcase and took the train to England.

Bluebell carried on working hard. A new troupe of Bluebell Girls was formed to work at the Casino in Monte Carlo for two months in the summer of 1946. There were eight dancers still appearing at the Chantilly until August 1947, when Bluebell's association there came to an end after five years. The Alhambra Music Hall in 1948 was another famous Paris theatre at which her dancers again appeared, billed as '*Les 12 Bluebells*' in shows which featured many of the post-war wave of new stars who were to dominate the entertainment business — the comedian Bourvil, the singer Yves Montand, the ballerina Ludmilla Tcherina, for instance.

The Bluebell Girls started to travel again, the China Theatre in Stockholm being one of their principal initial venues. Another troupe went to Italy in 1947, an appropriate destination since the last tour of the Bluebells outside France had taken place there in 1940. The Italian reaction was enthusiastic, and henceforth it was to be the most important European country other than France on the Bluebell circuit. There was a minor misjudgement at the start of the tour, when the girls danced in Milan. One of their appearances was a spectacular Spanish number, with swirling shawls, castanets and stamping feet. The first time they performed the audience began a barrage of hissing and booing. Bluebell suspected that it was because the girls were under-rehearsed, and the troupe worked overtime to polish up the number so that the next night it would be impeccable. Strangely, in spite of their efforts, the audience reaction was much the same. Finally a puzzled Bluebell was taken on one side by the management and given an explanation. It would seem that the Italians, remembering the friendliness between their late dictator Mussolini and General Franco, who had maintained Spanish neutrality through the war, and was still in power, held Spain in contempt. The number was instantly dropped and the tour continued, to approval and acclaim wherever the Bluebells played.

They also went north, into Scandinavia, and in Oslo caused a sensation, particularly among those Norwegians who could remember them playing there before the war. Everywhere the girls went in Norway it seemed as though they symbolized peacetime, a confirmation that the long war years were over, for the occupation of Norway did not end until the German defeat in May 1945. The Swedes in Gothenburg and Stockholm proved to be particularly enthusiastic.

In France peace was actually beginning to bite, in spite of the 'cold war' between the West and the Soviet bloc, which spawned, in Winston Churchill's memorable phrase, the Iron Curtain from the Baltic to the Black Sea. In 1947, Paris brilliantly reasserted its world supremacy in fashion when a young couturier, Christian Dior, brought forth his 'new look', a dramatic revolution on a major scale, achieving worldwide an alteration in the physical appearance of women. The severe, boxy, tailored look of the war and after was swept away in a flounce of frou-frou. Hemlines were lowered almost to the ankle, waists were as tightly pinched as they had been before the First World War by means of an effective miniature corset known as a 'waspie', and skirts were made as full as possible, with a shockingly profligate excess of material, and worn over several layers of frilled and frothy petticoats. Dior's genius lay in his sense of timing, and a shrewd realization that women were yearning, after so many years of hardship which had been reflected in their drab and austere wardrobes, for a return to femininity, and to blazes with emancipation, so he provided the means in an exaggerated form.

The 'new look' was naturally an influence on the costumes worn on stage, and the Bluebells' outfits accentuated certain elements of it, particularly the narrow waists. But as street clothes lengthened and women's legs returned to the virtual invisibility that was customary before the Twenties, when the last great fashion revolution had taken the world by storm, the Bluebells suddenly found that they had an enormous advantage now denied to the fashion-conscious women of Paris. Their legs, always long, shapely and magnificent, since Bluebell had determined that her girls should tower over

The first postwar Bluebells arrive in Monte Carlo, 1946

regular chorus girls in the mid-Thirties, now became a prized Parisian spectacle.

It was in 1947 that Mistinguett, allegedly well over seventy, and unpopular in France on account of her wartime record of consorting with the enemy, went to London and appeared on stage there, displaying a wrinkled visage but a still near-perfect pair of legs.

For Bluebell the most significant event of that year of 1947 was the birth, on 24th August, of her last child. He had actually arrived prematurely and was born at the country home, there being no time to get Bluebell back to Paris and the clinic where the other children had been born. The new arrival was her third son and he was christened Jean Paul George Kelly. Only the eldest, Patrick, did not carry Bluebell's adoptive name of Kelly. The Rue Blanche apartment was now hopelessly small, and as a matter of urgency she and Marcel had begun to look for a larger residence, which was a difficult undertaking in the conditions prevailing in Paris at that date. They needed to be located centrally, close to their places of work, since the lateness of their hours precluded lengthy nocturnal journeys into distant suburbs. But in their part of Paris there were no apartments for sale, and

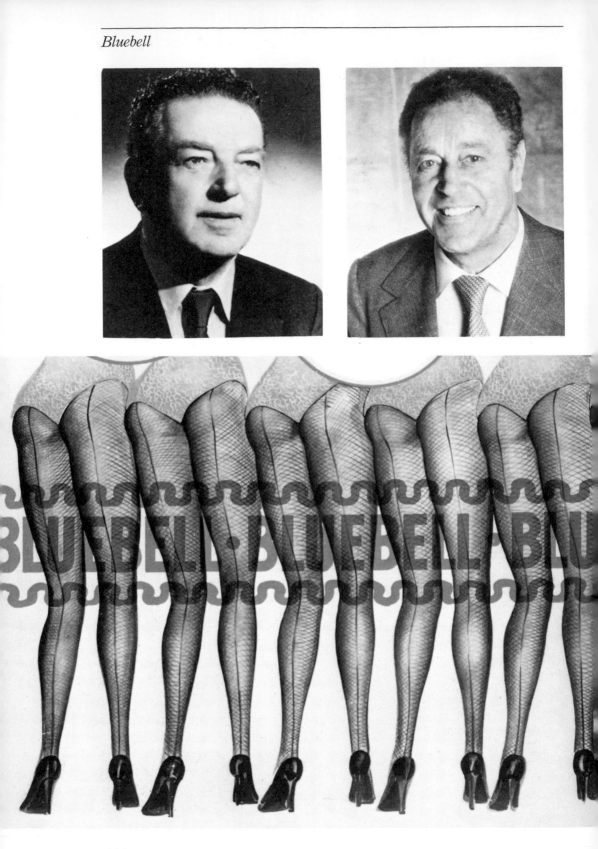

Left: Pierre Louis-Guérin

*Opposite page: masterminds of the Lido
Joseph (left) and Louis Clerico
Opposite page, below: a motif
from an Italian show brochure*

those that could be rented were only let to tenants who came up with exorbitant sums of so-called key money. There was no possibility that the Leibovicis were going to avoid this unpopular levy when the time came for them to move. But there would also have to be a big boost to their bank account, which, with four children and a nanny to support, was quite severely stretched.

The opportunity came in early 1948, when Bluebell went to have a drink on the spur of the moment at the Lido. There had been an earlier Lido, but it had now been replaced by a glittering new establishment. The new owners were brothers, Joseph and Louis Clerico, and they vowed that they would create a place of entertainment that would re-establish Paris as 'the city of light', the greatest night town in the world. They engaged Pierre Louis-Guérin to operate their new night club, which was ingeniously constructed in what had previously been swimming baths, and in spite of the problems of obtaining all the necessary building materials they managed to open up on schedule. It was an immediate success. The dowdy, run-down appearance of many of the famous pre-war theatres and cabarets had given a blighted look to the entertainment scene, and electricity shortages curtailed the once-celebrated street frontage displays of bright neon. The emergence of a sparkling new place to go to and be seen at in what had become a down-at-heel, shabby night-time scene brought back much of the old glamour, lacking in Paris for so long. The Clericos proved themselves to be shrewd judges of what was wanted, and like Dior had got their timing exactly right. By comparison with the Lido of today it was, in 1946, when they opened up, a relatively modest venture, but it stood head-and-shoulders above the others in business at the time.

Bluebell had long wanted to see just how successful it was, and that visit there with Marcel and two friends late one evening after the curtain had gone down at Les Ambassadeurs had a professional motive behind it. It was surprising that she had not heard of Guérin, because he undoubtedly had heard of her, and was most interested when one of the barmen came to his office and informed him that Madame Bluebell was in the bar with her husband and two friends enjoying a drink. It immediately stirred a thought that had been in his mind for some time. He told his informant to ask her if she would mind coming along to his office, as he would like to talk to her.

Guérin came straight to the point and asked Bluebell to come and work for him at the Lido. He wanted to improve the dancing in the show. As it happened he was already employing an ex-Bluebell dance captain from pre-war days, Dorothy Felton, and was well aware of the Bluebell style and reputation.

Bluebell responded with equal immediacy, and accepted on the spot. 'Good,' said Guérin. 'Come round tomorrow and we shall have a contract drawn up.' It was the beginning of an association with the Lido that has lasted for nearly forty years.

Meanwhile, Marcel left the Folies Bergère to be in charge of the orchestra for the new show being staged at the Pigalle. Unfortunately, its life was short, as is frequently the way in the performing world. He accepted its demise philosophically, and made the decision to enter into a full partnership with his wife, whose business was now beginning to grow extensively. Henceforth he would run the business and financial side of her operation, and made the forecast — not immodestly, given his considerable flair in that direction — that it would be only a matter of time before the Bluebell Girls were the most celebrated and prestigious dancing troupe in the world. He would also follow his primary calling, and provide all the orchestrations for the musical numbers for the tours, his skill as an arranger greatly adding to the marketable value of the Bluebells.

Bluebell had by now decided that conditions in Paris had eased sufficiently to bring back '*Les Anglaises*' — the English girls, who had always been so enormously popular on the continent. The new troupe she was forming for the Lido would have to be an extra-special one, and only the British could give her the quality she was seeking. So at the beginning of March 1948, having previously placed advertisements in *The Stage*, the weekly newspaper read by every aspirant to a career on the boards, she set sail for London to hold her auditions. There was no shortage of applicants. Bluebell's quest received extensive publicity in the newspapers, which, although still hampered by rigorous newsprint rationing that kept them short of pages, never needed excuses to print photographs of attractive young women, and were able to find them in droves lining up to demonstrate their talents in front of the legendary Miss Bluebell. She quickly and efficiently whittled the hopefuls down to a shortlist, and then finally decided

Top: the Kelly Boys. Above: Bluebells backstage at the Lido, 1950

on the lucky few who would be travelling to France a few days later. They were due to make their debut at the Lido on 1st April, so time for settling in and starting rehearsals would be very limited.

The beginnings at the Lido were on a relatively small scale. The first Bluebells to travel out from Britain in post-war years made up a tiny group, consisting of only eight girls. But in addition to them there were four male dancers — the beginnings of her new troupe, the Kelly Boys. In April 1948 the new show opened, performed each night at 11 p.m., after two hours of dinner and dancing for the Lido patrons. There was room in the huge, cavernous room to seat 800 people for dinner, with a dance floor that at show time would be converted into a stage capable of supporting elaborate scenic effects.

The first show in which the Bluebell dancers appeared, actually the third to be staged at the Clericos' Lido, was called *Confetti*. In that post-war period Lido shows would normally be budgeted to run for six months at first, but this period was later extended to a year. The tall, poised, statuesque Bluebells, with their white skin and dazzling smiles, made such a favourable impression with the Lido's clientele that there was no hesitation on Guérin's part when it came to renewing their contract for the 1949 revue, which was called *Bravo*.

Earlier, in the summer of 1948, three months after *Confetti* had opened, Bluebell received word from Liverpool that Mary Murphy was seriously ill in hospital. She immediately cancelled her current engagements and caught the next boat train to England, hastening north to be at her bedside. It seemed clear that the old lady had very little time left, but her indomitable will kept her going for much longer than the doctors had expected. The vigil extended into days, a week, two weeks, but Mary Murphy, although weak and tired, lingered on. Bluebell became anxious about her responsibilities in Paris, where the livelihoods of many people depended on her presence. Finally, one of the doctors, sensing her dilemma, took her on one side and told her that it might be months before Mary Murphy died, and that Bluebell might just as well go back to France, since there was little that she could do in Liverpool. Relieved on the one hand, but reluctant on the other, she returned to the Lido. The following day her Liverpool cousin, George Kelly, sent her a telegram to say that Mary Murphy had died shortly after her departure. Bluebell telephoned him. He told her that there really was no need for her to go back, as he would handle all the arrangements and see to it that the old lady had a decent funeral. Her little cottage in Mercer Place, behind her original home in Deysbrook Lane, was later stripped bare, but Bluebell, immersed in her work at the Lido, and catching up on her protracted absence, failed to remember until it was too late that there were many precious photographs, letters and other items that had been in Mary Murphy's possession, including the famous pre-war Folies Bergère programmes on which the embarrassed woman had inked in bras and

Patrick, Jean Paul, Francis, Florence, Marcel and Bluebell at home in the Rue Marbeuf

panties over the *mannequins nues*. All such things were to vanish for ever.

In Paris the Lcibovicis had found a new apartment, in the excellent residential district of Rue Marbeuf, a narrow street linking Avenue George V with the Avenue des Champs-Elysées, thus forming the bottom side of a triangle. By Rue Blanche standards the new home at 27 Rue Marbeuf was a palace, a huge nine-roomed flat with sufficient space to accommodate the four children and Paulette, the nanny, in comfort, with room still left over for occasional guests. It did not, however, come cheaply. As well as the considerable rent, Marcel and Bluebell had to provide some thirty thousand francs in key money, an 'under the table' payment which ensured that the place would be theirs. Even with bank loans it was necessary to find extra finance, so although they had only owned their second country house in Normandy for two years they sold it, resolving to look for somewhere else in that favourite part of the French countryside, which was so easily accessible from Paris, when their finances had overcome the shock of moving.

Even after they had paid the large sum of key money a snag still arose. The apartment was left empty to enable redecorating to be carried out, and the Leibovicis continued to live at the Rue Blanche, having given in their notice to quit. One day Marcel, visiting the Rue Marbeuf, discovered that his key did not work — the lock had been changed. On further investigation it was found that the famous couturier, Jacques Fath, had moved in with his cutting tables and a twenty-strong team of cutters and seamstresses, and in effect had turned the place into workrooms for his business. Clearly there had been some double-dealing going on. Bluebell, aghast and terrified that shortly they would have nowhere to live, confided in Guérin at the Lido. His response was prompt. He telephoned a high-ranking police officer he happened to know and explained the situation. Jacques Fath's workers were evicted within twenty-four hours. Bluebell never met Fath, and certainly never wore any of his creations, deeming them 'far too expensive!'

Apart from its spaciousness the Rue Marbeuf apartment was extremely handy for the Lido, which was only two or three minutes walk away, on the

Gary Cooper meets the Bluebells

Donn Arden, from America with ideas   *René Fraday, Lido artistic director*

other side of the Champs-Elysées. Normally it was a pleasant enough stroll except when the weather was against it, and in the late Forties the traffic on the famous thoroughfare was still at a reasonable level, so that crossing the road on foot was not such a suicide mission as it is today. Bluebell took her time organizing the move, taking advantage of the fact that the two apartments were leased simultaneously, thus giving her the time to get the new place decorated and furnished to her taste. It was to serve not only as a residence but also as an office, and it would be the world headquarters of the Bluebell organization. Ever since her first days in charge of the girls at the Paramount she had worked out of home, preferring the independence such an arrangement entailed, rather than basing herself in an office at the Lido. To this day she has persisted in that custom, and regards it as having many advantages, not least the provision of a neutral ground away from the pressure of the backstage area, so that the dancers could see her to discuss any personal difficulties with no fear of intervention by the management. It also reinforced their sense of being employees of Miss Bluebell, rather than of the Lido, or whichever other theatre in which they happened to be working long-term.

The number of dancers under her wing began to increase. As the Forties came to an end the Bluebell Girls had already become a permanent attraction at the Lido, just as they had been at the pre-war Folies Bergère. For the 1950 show, *Enchantment*, there were now sixteen of them, plus the troupes on tour. She and Marcel were soon making regular visits to England to engage new talent, and the national newspapers, at a time when almost all manufactured luxury goods had to be sent overseas for the sake of the

171

desperate balance of payments crisis, were saying that the Bluebell Girls were on a par with Scotch whisky as one of the most important exports from Britain. Henceforth she was to select up to ninety per cent of the girls there, always ensuring that they were all more than 5ft 9in tall.

The Lido was a place for Americans, not only as tourists but backstage as well. Guérin liked to engage acts that would give the cabaret a fully international flavour. Among them was a young dancer in a team called the Debonairs. His name was Douglas Scott. When the run of *Confetti* ended he stayed behind and joined the production staff who staged the shows, eventually becoming responsible for putting the performances on every night as the Lido's stage manager, a post he held until he returned to America at the end of 1984.

Something about the Lido seemed to encourage longevity. The artistic director, René Fraday, began there in that extraordinary post-war period, and is perhaps the chief architect for the style of presentation to this day. There was also Donn Arden, who had been working in the entertainment business in Las Vegas since 1938, and was now engaged by the Lido to stage his spectacular shows. His special genius was in the creation of elaborate and breathtaking set-pieces, using a wide variety of materials and designing backdrops and stage areas which would show off the dancers to the best advantage. The audience would then be dazzled with a combination of light, movement and sound. Guérin did not regard his productions as showcases for stars but let the show itself be the star, and they were organized to zip along at a rapid pace, offering the audience a feeling that their money had been well spent. Donn Arden's fame increased in Las Vegas at a greater rate than in Paris, where a very modest programme credit was the only acknowledgement of his involvement, but throughout the years his work at the Lido has given him as much satisfaction as that in the United States.

These post-war years represented the most fruitful part of Bluebell's professional career, for the Lido gave her the opportunity to develop her special skills as the director of a group of dancers.

She may not have been the greatest choreographer in the world, but she knew the importance of presentation and discipline, and encouraged her dancers to make the most of themselves. She also was quick to appreciate that changes had occurred in dancing techniques since the days of the pre-war Folies. The Americans, in particular, had evolved a new style of modern dance, first on Broadway, with the Agnes de Mille ballet in *Oklahoma!* forming a major landmark. It spread to Hollywood, to be seen in many of the great post-war musicals of MGM under the aegis of Arthur Freed, including *On The Town* and *An American in Paris*, both starring Gene Kelly, and *The Band Wagon* with Fred Astaire. Bluebell saw and loved these films and they influenced the shows at the Lido. The old precision lines of high-kicking legs, the mainstay of performances of the Alfred Jackson Girls, would be insufficient to satisfy a modern Lido audience. For the Bluebells themselves

Bluebell and the Girls, 1948

it meant that the dancing was more difficult but also more interesting.

Bluebell's power became considerable, and her involvement in the planning of new shows started at the very beginning. To the girls she was both a boss and a mother figure, and she was able to command their confidence and respect, even though she worked them hard and expected high standards at all times. To the Lido administration she was an important cog in the smooth-running machine, which was geared to be open for business on 365 days of the year. The Lido was one of the great success stories of post-war Paris, with Bluebell playing as large a part in it as the rest of her management.

It would be pleasant to record that all was well during this exciting period of expansion and fulfilment, but it would be inaccurate. For although the business relationship ran smoothly and successfully, the personal side did not. Marcel's constant womanizing became a burden and the cause for pain. It was particularly demoralizing when he was conducting an affair with one of the Bluebells themselves, and such situations called for enormous reserves of control on Bluebell's part. She never fired a girl, or even disciplined her as a consequence of being involved with her husband. Instead, she retained her dignity, as much for the morale of the company as for her own, and publicly never even acknowledged what was going on. But such stoicism could only be achieved at a price, and once she admitted to herself that Marcel was fatally flawed, the damage to their relationship was deep and lasting.

13   Las Vegas Nights

NEVADA ATTRACTED GAMBLERS even in the nineteenth century. Prospectors on their way to California chanced their hand in the desert hills and occasionally hit veins of silver. Where diggings had produced results rapid communities of wooden huts would spring up, only to be abandoned soon after when the initial optimism had died, leaving dozens of ghost towns and abandoned shafts across the state.

One such nondescript place was called Las Vegas, but it was destined to have an advantage which would set it apart from the rest. The Union Pacific Railroad had decided in 1905 to build a depot there, and almost overnight the dusty desert acres were transformed into highly desirable building lots for a proper town. The presence of a railroad stop was to ensure that Las Vegas would outlast brief mining booms, and become a town of some permanence.

It was still not much of a place until the Thirties, when the rest of the United States was in the grip of the Depression. In 1931 the state legislature of Nevada made gambling legal — it had been going on for years more or less openly anyway — and casinos were able to open up in the downtown area where Fremont and Main Streets crossed. Meanwhile, work began

The Bluebells reach the Wild West

nearby on one of the most spectacular and ambitious engineering feats of the twentieth century, the monumental dam on the Colorado River, which was initially named after the adjacent workers' dormitory town of Boulder, but was later, in 1947, formally designated with the name of the American president under whose aegis the project had begun — Hoover. Its intention was to irrigate and provide hydro-electric power for several western states which hitherto had endured annual devastation from the vicious flooding of the Colorado when the Rocky Mountain snows melted.

The building of the Hoover Dam meant that immediately two enormous benefits accrued to Las Vegas. In the first instance the thousands of migrants who made up the labour force, and whose pockets on payday bulged with unaccustomed high earnings, were lured by the bright casino lights of the glittering city less than twenty-five miles up the highway, where temptation awaited to take advantage of man's natural greed. The other boon was the creation of the vast resort area of Lake Mead, the huge man-made body of water created behind the dam, which was completed in 1935. From what had earlier been spectacular but inhospitable desert grew a welcoming tourist centre, offering boating, swimming, fishing, camping, riding and trailing all within half-an-hour's drive from Las Vegas.

Then came the war and an increase in migration to the west as the weapons and aircraft factories, less fettered for space than in the crowded

east, sprang up, bringing in fresh influxes of well-paid workers. Demobbed GIs decided to move out west and Las Vegas became a way station for the great early post-war Californian boom, which transformed areas in and around Los Angeles such as the San Fernando Valley and Orange County. Before the war the gambling capital of the United States had been Reno, but now Las Vegas acquired the crown. It was actually nearer to Los Angeles, with its rapidly-increasing population, than to its Nevada neighbour in the north-west.

The ending of gasoline rationing meant that new hotels with casinos and vast parking lots could come into existence. The first was the huge Flamingo, which was built in record time by Bugsy Siegel, an east coast gangster who had moved west. However, he was murdered in 1946 at his home in Beverly Hills, before he could benefit from the success of the hotel, which went on to prosper after his death. Other establishments followed and began to outvie each other in the brilliance of the floor shows they were able to offer. The entertainments were the magnets to entice people into the casinos, and were reached only after the audience had threaded its way past the tables and the slot machines. Top-line stars were soon being paid gigantic fees to appear before packed audiences, who had been attracted to Las Vegas by reasonable room rates and meal prices. Accommodation and food there is cheap because the main income comes from gambling. There

177

are a myriad ways in which money can be extracted by managements from visitors throughout the whole twenty-four hours of a day.

The basic symbol of Las Vegas is the slot machine, which is ubiquitous and inescapable. Rows of them are first to be sighted at the airport. No hotel lobby is bereft of them and they can even be found in many of the washrooms.

The brilliantly lit 'Strip' came into existence, officially Las Vegas Boulevard South, a thoroughfare which proved to be an attractive location for the huge new post-war hotels, each fronted by a gigantic neon sign with a 'marquee', an area where the names of the celebrity performers are displayed as prominently as man's ingenuity will allow. The Flamingo, the Desert Inn, the Sands, the Dunes, the Riviera, the Sahara and many others jostled for attention along the gaudy boulevard — they would later be joined by Caesars' Palace, Circus Circus with its unabashed child appeal, and the monumental MGM Grand, while the Hilton Corporation acquired their largest international hotel in Las Vegas.

It is one of the strangest cities in the world. The prime industry is gambling, and millions of people flock there each year for that purpose. The airport, only three miles from the centre of town, handles nearly twelve million passengers a year, putting it well ahead of most major American cities. The casinos are windowless and clockless, air-conditioned against the dry desert heat outside, and the action at the tables carries on around the clock. At dusk Las Vegas, when viewed from two or three miles off, looks like some futuristic space colony, certainly like nowhere else on earth. At night it blazes with millions of light bulbs and thousands of miles of neon tubing, and sometimes the glare can be discerned in the desert sky more than a hundred miles away.

Although its alleged Mafia connections are legendary it is a surprisingly orderly place. The gambling is not crooked. The Nevada Gaming Board exerts considerable muscle on the conduct of operations, and while the visitor is almost certain to lose a lot of money if he indulges, it will not be because the casino has cheated him, but because the odds are officially loaded in their favour. However, after the unwary punter has been skinned he can always go and have a 49 cent breakfast (some places offer such absurdly cheap meals as an inducement) and then marry a rich widow, since instant weddings, permissible under Nevada law, are a secondary, but very profitable Las Vegas industry.

The shows at the hotels became increasingly spectacular during the post-war years and the Fifties. In 1955 the Royal Nevada began the idea of importing Broadway musicals by staging *Guys and Dolls*, and now Las Vegas invariably provides a platform for national companies. From the hits of Broadway to the spectacles of Paris was but a short hop. In 1958 Frank Sennes, at the newly-built Stardust, which until the Hilton was opened was the biggest of the hotels there, decided to bring in the show from the Paris

Lido, giving it some extra Vegan flourishes. The Lido has been a fixture there ever since, having been seen by more than twenty million people. The idea was quickly copied, so that the Folies Bergère became associated with the Tropicana and the Moulin Rouge with the Hilton. The Stardust show broke new ground in that it was not just to be the sumptuous backing for a star, but a show in its own right, without a headline performer taking centre stage. The lavish revue format, while traditional in Paris, was at that time unknown in Las Vegas, and was another way in which the Stardust was to lead the way there. Billed quite accurately as 'direct from Paris', the Lido at the Stardust aroused an anticipatory sensation even before it had opened.

The Bluebells were, of course, to be an integral part of the new show. During the Fifties they had been touring all over the world as well as being permanently associated with the Lido in Paris and all the productions that were staged there. It was decided that there was a powerful publicity advantage to be derived from the invasion of America by a troupe of beautiful, statuesque, mostly British girls, whose height made them prominent in any crowd. Accordingly, Bluebell, making her first visit to the United States, flew to New York with her selected group, all of whom had worked in the Paris shows and had volunteered to cross the Atlantic. The airline's public relations team ensured that the press was out in force as the Super-Constellation from Paris landed at Idlewild (now JFK) Airport in Jamaica, New York, and on the principle that few excuses are needed by editors to print pictures of pretty girls they achieved considerable coverage in the eastern newspapers. After a few days of interviews with the press, radio and television, they took off for Nevada, arriving at McCarran Airport, Las Vegas to more flashlights and publicity.

The Stardust production had been fully rehearsed in Paris before the journey to the United States, with Donn Arden and several Americans who were either appearing in or associated with it flying over to take part. Even so, the first few days after their arrival in Nevada were strained for Bluebell. She recalls how once rehearsals had started there — and as usual, in spite of the extensive preparations in Paris, there was still the same breathtaking rush that there always is — her girls experienced considerable problems in adjusting to the climate, which ranged from 120° heat outside in the sun to polar conditions in the air-conditioned indoors. The first and biggest battle she fought concerned the public conduct of the girls themselves. Las Vegas has a reputation for being a broad-minded town, and what its guests get up to is of little concern to anybody unless it constitutes a public nuisance. That the Bluebells should be seen to be smartly dressed offstage went without saying — Bluebell always encouraged good appearances. But it was suggested that it would be a splendid idea for them to mingle with the customers when they were not on stage, and to sit at their tables.

In lesser establishments chorus girls sometimes extended their earnings by granting favours, and thus, in essence, became prostitutes. Bluebell was

The Bluebells in 1955 and overleaf at the end of the decade

adamant that her girls were not to be exposed to such risks, even though she faced the hard-faced, tough bosses who ran Vegas and behaved as though they were in a bad Hollywood gangster movie. She threatened to walk out and take the whole of her team back to Paris if such conditions were imposed, and her anger made it perfectly clear that she meant what she said. It was something that the Bluebells never did, anywhere, and there were absolutely no exceptions. 'But we would like it!' said one of the hard men. 'Bluebells don't do that!' Bluebell snapped back. The man was clearly not accustomed to being on the wrong side of the argument, and even Bluebell later had a sleepless night.

But by digging in her heels on this issue the message was hammered home. The following day she was summoned to a meeting of the top hierarchy, and was given an apology and an assurance that her views would be honoured. She was so astonished that when she was offered a drink she ordered a Coca-Cola, in spite of the fact that she never drank the stuff. The decision was conclusive. Bluebells would not be required to mix with the gambling patrons after the show. The bosses had retreated and she had managed to get her way. Had she not the show would not have opened, so she had held the upper hand, although she would have found herself considerably out of pocket, since she would have been liable for the air fares of the company back to Europe. But it was perhaps naïve of the management to imagine that they could get the better of a woman whose stubborn and indomitable attitude had not even been cracked by the Germans during the wartime occupation of France.

But later, when she was back in Paris, they tried to get their revenge on Bluebell. She was asked by Pierre Louis-Guérin to see him and he said, 'Miss, we have a problem. They want to prolong the show for a year — but they don't want you.' Bluebell said, 'That's no problem.' One of the Clerico brothers then said, 'But what do we do about the girls?' 'That'll be your problem, not mine,' said Bluebell. Thus was she able to assert herself and make it clear that with no Bluebell there would be no Bluebells.

Obviously, this was only one side of the Las Vegas experience. The show, which Donn Arden, who was brought in from the Desert Inn and was working on his home territory, directed, was fashioned out of various elements of past Lido shows, with the addition of several original items. It was a huge hit, and for a time the Stardust was the envy of the other hotels along the Strip, who jostled for ways of emulating such success.

The run of the first show was extended from six months to one year, and Bluebell was invited to return to Las Vegas to start the arrangements for the succeeding production. When she arrived at the Stardust she found a bottle of champagne waiting for her in her suite and a note from the man with whom she had been in altercation. He apologized for being out of town but told her to call his secretary to ensure that she had everything she wanted, and no expense was to be spared.

It has always been one of Bluebell's most formidable characteristics to defend her girls with a fierce, staunch authority. It is not simply her humanitarianism — there is a sound business reason behind her attitude. From the start she was determined that her troupes should be the elite of dancers, and that in spite of the glamour, exposure and sexuality of their stage appearance there would be nothing cheap or sleazy about the girls themselves. It would be absurd to suggest that they never went out with members of the audience. But any arrangements made would be achieved through the girls' own ingenuity and would not be with Bluebell's approval. The rule has always been to behave with discretion and good taste, and not advertise liaisons. But a surprisingly large proportion of Bluebells found husbands in America, particularly among men who worked in Las Vegas itself, and settled there to raise daughters who in turn became second-generation Bluebell dancers.

An example of Bluebell's obdurate protective sense towards her girls occurred in 1958, when some of her dancers were appearing for the first time in India, at Prince's Oberoi Grand in Calcutta. On the opening night Bluebell was horrified to hear, as the Bluebells were announced, one of a group of eight English people among the diners say, in a voice redolent of alcoholic exuberance: 'Bill! Why don't we go and dance with the girls?' As he made his way down the stairs to the dance floor Bluebell barred his way. 'Get back to your seat!' she ordered in her toughest manner. 'Who are you?' he mumbled. 'Never mind who I am — get back to your table.' Meekly he went back and watched the show. Afterwards he came and apologized, and thanked Bluebell for preventing him from making a fool of himself. 'I brought this show all the way from Paris,' she said, 'and I wasn't going to let you destroy it.' But it was sheer good fortune that had caused her to be in the right place at that crucial moment.

By the end of the Fifties the Bluebells were truly a world organization. Their base in Paris was complemented by the now permanent troupe in Las

Vegas, while at any given moment some part of the world — Europe, Africa, the Far East — would be on the touring schedule. Television, too, became an important medium. The girls had first appeared on the small screen in the pioneering days before the war, when the French broadcasting authority set up an experimental service transmitted from the Eiffel Tower. In 1950 the BBC featured the Bluebells on the then single British channel, in programmes of continental cabaret. Later RAI, the Italian broadcasting organization, regularly featured the Bluebell dancers as backing for variety shows and for a weekly series with the comedian Walter Chiari.

During this sustained period of business expansion Marcel, although increasingly distant from Bluebell as a husband, maintained a firm grip on the development of their joint interests, as well as being a firm and attentive father to the four children, who were growing up. The eldest, Patrick, was at university, when on 27th March 1961, while he was being driven by his father back to Paris from a visit to the south of France, the car left the road and hit a bridge.

'I had a group at the Palais Méditerranée in Nice, and some problem had arisen there,' said Bluebell. 'He had taken Patrick with him as he was on vacation from the university. Marcel phoned me at nine o'clock on the evening before, and told me that he would be back before I was up the next morning. And then at six o'clock the children came in and woke me, and said that there had been an accident.' The police had come to the Rue Marbeuf apartment to break the news.

Bluebell telephoned Pierre Louis-Guérin and told him what had happened, and both hurriedly dressed to rush to the hospital at Sens, where they had been taken. There she was told that her husband was dead. Bluebell was astonished to find that he lay unmarked, while Patrick, who was alive, was bloody and puffy-faced from his injuries, and looked as though he had been through a far worse ordeal.

An early Sixties photocall for the Bluebells

The theory was that Marcel, legendarily a fast driver, had fallen asleep while driving his latest Citroën and the car had struck the abutment of the bridge, Patrick in the passenger seat being hurled into a field. No other cars were involved in the accident.

Many believed that the death of Marcel would mark the end of the Bluebells. It was generally accepted that he was the motive force behind their commercial success, and that without him Bluebell would be unable to continue. Not only was she now wholly responsible for the four children, but there were two of Marcel's sisters who had to be looked after. But Bluebell, once she had recovered from the shock of her sudden widowhood, decided that she would carry on. She was, after all, still relatively young at forty-eight and there were a large number of people in her employ who depended on her for their livelihood. But it was not an easy matter to unravel the complexities of Marcel's arrangements of Bluebell's affairs, which usually required his signature rather than hers. Years later, when she was moving out of the Rue Marbeuf apartment, she found that it was still registered in his name, even though she had been paying the rent consistently for a long time.

Her strength of character, as so often in the past, asserted itself. She decided that what she did not know about accounting, contracts, terms of employment, she would learn — fast. There were lawyers to deal with, and complex business matters to unravel. She was now on her own and had to choose very carefully those people in whom she felt she could place her trust. It was an intensely pragmatic period, made no easier by the necessity to keep the Bluebells' programme going, and suddenly, in addition to her already crowded personal schedule, she was obliged to assume fresh burdens. She had heard the gossip, and that had acted as a spur. She was determined to prove the gossips wrong, and to show that the Bluebells could carry on and prosper, even though Marcel was no longer behind her. But then, all her life, she had never been able to resist a challenge. Patrick, who was due for military service as soon as he had graduated from the Sorbonne, was able to make a plea to the authorities not to be sent overseas, and was instead given a posting near Paris which enabled him to go home frequently and help his mother.

A year or two before Marcel was killed they had engaged a manager in Britain, whose job was to look for and audition new dancers. 'I needed someone resident in Britain to take care of the licensing. When you take a girl under eighteen out of the country on a job you have to have a licence. A girl who was coming to work with me told me about Peter Baker, who seemed to know the business very well,' said Bluebell. Peter Baker still fulfils this function after more than twenty-five years, and from his office and studio on the seafront at Worthing interviews hundreds of potential Bluebells every year, often seeing them when they are still at school, and clearly too young to be engaged. His presence greatly eases the pressures

Above: Bluebell leads a rehearsal
Below: last moment adjustments

187

facing Bluebell when she makes her regular journeys to England to recruit new dancers, as the hardest part of the work has already been done by the time she gets there. Many of the girls were originally trained to be ballet dancers, but were unable to continue because they were too tall; in any case, Peter Baker believes that, with the exception of the Royal Ballet, dance teaching in Britain is fifty years behind the times. In more recent years, given the awakening in public interest in dance as a pleasant alternative to the more mundane ways of keeping fit, there have been improvements.

Bluebell remained at the Rue Marbeuf for eleven years after Marcel's death, living there for twenty-four years in all. It had been a good place in which to bring up the children, although there had been moments when the neighbours had threatened intervention, particularly when they engaged in fierce pillow fights during their parents' nocturnal absences. By the Seventies they had all grown up, and she felt that the time had come to find somewhere more suitable — a flat that would be more compact and easier to manage. She found a penthouse apartment in a newly-built block in the Rue de la Faisanderie, a narrow street leading off the Avenue Foch and close to the Porte Dauphine. It is in one of the most sought-after areas of Paris, much favoured by diplomats and senior professionals, yet within a few minutes of the Lido, and with a convenient taxi *tête de station* by the Métro station on the corner, a minute away from the spacious and airy lobby of her building.

As has always been her custom Bluebell conducts her business from the apartment, there being an office adjoining her spacious sitting-room which has a western aspect picture-window looking out across the rooftops towards the Bois de Boulogne. Each afternoon her secretary Michèle Wormser arrives to deal with the myriad matters that are constantly arising in the organization — contracts, replacements, schedules, travel arrangements, auditions, correspondence — while the telephone rings more or less constantly.

Bluebells begins her day relatively late for normal people, at around noon, and devotes her full energies to business matters as soon as she has had a light lunch. Unless she has to go early to the Lido for rehearsals she remains in the flat dealing with the backlog of paperwork, and talking on the telephone. She will switch from a mundane call about replacing a girl who has gone down with flu for that night's show to arranging the opening night for a team about to appear in Korea, then to a (for him) dawn call from Donn Arden in California to discuss a forthcoming date in Las Vegas. And in the early evening, when Michèle has gone, she prepares to go to the Lido, getting there usually by eight-thirty, and not leaving until three in the morning or later, to be ready for the following day.

Donn Arden is a lifelong bachelor, but also one of her oldest friends. He first went into show business as a youth, and was involved in mounting shows in the gambling casinos which existed in Florida and New York. He

New Year's celebrations at the Lido, Bluebell with Donn Arden

quickly discovered why hardly any of the people who work in such places gamble. The lure of the slot machines and the tables was compulsive, and after a while he found that he owed rather more than his annual salary in gambling debts. From then on, he jokes, he could never leave the business, as the syndicate insisted that he pay off every penny, however long it took. It took him two years and put him off gambling for life.

His show at the Riviera, New York came to an end when the building was demolished for a freeway along the banks of the Hudson, and he decided to move permanently to the west coast. He had first mounted a show in Las Vegas at the Desert Inn in 1950, and claims that ever since he has never had less than one running in the town. He became world-renowned for the brilliance of his Las Vegas entertainments, and developed the techniques for spectacle and special effects that brought him into great demand.

He first met Bluebell when she started at the Lido in 1948. He had been brought over to bring his special skills to the shows that were being staged there in its new, post-war incarnation. 'At that time Bluebell looked like a very round, blonde, Betty Grable–June Haver type of girl. We met and talked and she showed me Gay Paree — I knew nothing about Pigalle and Montmartre, and she was even living up there. We hit it off. But we had some arguments. She had her ways from the Folies Bergère days and the Paramount theatre, but I had my ways, too, like a definite New York way

189

of dressing the girls and the colours we used, and even our dance forms. We argue a lot, but we're very good friends, and we're good for one another. We generally come out with a good product.'

Such a philosophy is perfectly in tune with Bluebell, who believes that it is unhealthy not to argue. 'A good argument can do the world of good!'

The transplanting of the Lido style of presentation to Las Vegas was the fulfilment of one of Donn Arden's dreams. He is also the man who introduced the topless showgirl to Las Vegas audiences. Hitherto nudes on the American stage had only been associated with burlesque theatres, which were predominantly patronized by males and for the most part only to be found in sleazy sections of large cities. Donn Arden, like Florenz Ziegfeld and Paul Derval before him, unveiled the tasteful nude, and presented bare breasts with jewels, feathers, furs and expensive trappings in the midst of exotic Paris-style revues at Las Vegas. With the passage of the years the length of the shows' runs has steadily increased. In the beginning the first show was expected to last six months, then a year's run became norm, then two, and the current show at the Stardust has lasted more than six years. By the time the Stardust celebrated its silver jubilee in 1983 it had hosted thirteen Lido shows, but the majority of them had been in the earlier years.

But the Stardust, a sensation when it was built in the late Fifties, was due to be eclipsed with the next generation of Las Vegas hotels, and in particular the building that was to be erected on the site near the corner of the Strip and Flamingo Road, partly occupied by the small Bonanza Hotel.

14   **Inferno**

KIRK KERKORIAN, A strangely reticent Las Vegas billionaire, made an enormous fortune selling a hotel he acquired, the Flamingo, and one he built, the International, to the Hilton chain, and in the early Seventies, using capital from the sale of various assets of the Metro-Goldwyn-Mayer studios in Culver City, to the horror both of the shareholders and of those who regarded MGM as the *ne plus ultra* of Hollywood majors, he financed a new resort which was to be the largest hotel–casino complex in the world.

It was to be called the MGM Grand Hotel, recalling the title of one of the studio's most successful films of the Thirties, and the ground-breaking ceremony took place on the corner of Flamingo Road and the Strip on 15th April 1972, on a site where the Bonanza, which Kerkorian had acquired, had lately stood. Guests, including Cary Grant, Betty Grable and Janet Leigh, watched Raquel Welch press a plunger, which blasted off a dynamite charge and started a magnificent display of fireworks, including a pyrotechnic rendering of the famous MGM 'Leo the Lion' logo.

Nineteen months later the enormous building, twenty-six storeys high, offering two-and-a-half million square feet of space on its T-shaped floor plan, was receiving its first guests. It was Christmas Eve, 1974. Among the

191

many attractions was a casino larger than a football field, over 2,000 guest rooms, each with a star on the door, six restaurants and three theatres, one of them dedicated to showing mint-condition prints from the vaults of MGM's classic movies, another the 1,400-seat Celebrity Room, which would always feature a top star (the opening performer was Dean Martin), and the Ziegfeld Room, the home of a spectacular show masterminded by Donn Arden, using all his ingenuity and the resources of a stage area on which millions of dollars had been lavished.

The show there was billed as Donn Arden's *Hallelujah Hollywood,* and its enormous cast included over a hundred dancers and showgirls, performing in a rapidly paced spectacular revue which paid tribute to the great musicals of MGM's history, such as *Meet Me in St Louis* and *Singin' in the Rain.* The programme credit for the supervision of the vast company of MGM Girls who danced through the numbers went to Margaret Kelly. Contractually she was not allowed to use the name Bluebell at the MGM Grand, as that was for the Stardust, where the Bluebells were billed on the marquee.

But the new show at the MGM was the most elaborate yet seen, even in Las Vegas, and was a major factor in producing a $22 million profit for the Grand Hotel in its first trading year, in a business in which break-even point in itself would be a major achievement in such a short time.

Kerkorian's hotel seemed to be an unbridled success, and a similar structure on the same gigantic scale was planned and constructed at Reno, eventually opening for business in 1978.

The cost of *Hallelujah Hollywood* was so great that it had to run for years to recoup its costs, and it was in fact to last for six. After the Reno show had been launched Donn Arden began a two-year period of preparation on the successor to *Hallelujah Hollywood,* which was to be even more spectacular, and very likely to cost over $10 million. It was to be called *Jubilee.* Bluebell flew over from Paris to work with him, and to audition, assemble and rehearse the dancers. *Hallelujah Hollywood* closed on 12th October 1980 and the new show went into rehearsal, to be ready for its December opening, in time for the Christmas holidays.

'We were going incredibly well,' said Donn Arden, 'and I had never been so far ahead before — we could almost have opened early.'

On 20th November the show had an excellent run-through, with everyone knowing their cues, and all that was left to be worked out were the technical effects on the stage of the Ziegfeld. Many of the cast members were in a celebratory mood, and although the rehearsal had finished late they went off to various parties. Donn Arden and Bluebell retired to their rooms on the tenth floor to get some well-earned rest.

The following morning at 7.15 the ground floor of the enormous hotel was as quiet as it was ever likely to be during the course of its twenty-four-hour day. Unlike in a typical urban business hotel, few guests would be breakfasting or checking out for an early flight, and the morning rush was

Upfront diners eye the Bluebells

Above: Bluebell and Douglas Scott   *Right: Bluebell and Donn Arden*

not expected for another hour. At the blackjack tables one or two long-night gamblers still lingered, while in the coin cages the takings of the previous busy night were being counted. Suddenly a woman kitchen worker came running out of the New York Deli, a restaurant next to the coffee shop where a day-long menu of lox, pastrami, borscht and blintzes was always available. She yelled to a security guard that the Deli kitchen was on fire. He reacted at once, and immediately alerted his colleagues, one of whom told the switchboard operator to call the Las Vegas fire department. Kitchen fires in hotels are not uncommon, but must always be treated seriously, so two fire stations immediately sent out engines, as well as a paramedic ambulance team which was based only half a minute away, on the other side of the street.

There were no alarms set off in the hotel, and people were still piling coins into the slot machines as helmeted firemen ran into the lobby, which was by now becoming noticeably smoky. Then tragedy struck. In front of the Deli the ceiling suddenly burst into flames. The firefighters frantically screamed to clear everyone off the ground floor, and a few startled people managed to escape in time. But a fireball swept through the length of the lobby in seconds, igniting the casino, and continued right out into the main entrance and forecourt, devastating everything in its wake. The carpets, chandeliers, tables and chairs erupted in flame. Fourteen people died in the instantaneous holocaust in the casino, while thousands more in the rest of the hotel were now threatened by carbon monoxide and cyanide gases seeping into the ducts from the melted plastic fittings and wall coverings. Outside a column of smoke soared thousands of feet into the sky, and emergency units were racing to the hotel from every direction.

Astonishingly, some of the guests in the hotel, which was full, first learned that it was on fire as they were watching the ABC breakfast programme, *Good Morning America*, being transmitted live from New York. Others heard a commotion and left their rooms to investigate only to find that they could not get back. The hotel switchboard was unusable after 7.20 a.m., by which time its components had succumbed to the heat, but the internal telephones went on working for another hour.

The fire engines gathered around the hotel and loudspeakers were used to tell people to stay in their rooms until they could be rescued. For the people in the upper floors that instruction seemed to pose questions, for the

longest escape ladder could only reach to the ninth storey of the building. Many people managed to open or break their windows, and were pathetically dangling sheets and blankets from them, although there was not a hope of reaching the ground except in a fall. The nightmare the firemen now faced was that the flames would engulf the elevator shafts, and set the bedroom wings of the hotel alight. There would be no way to control such a conflagration and a death toll in the thousands would be the result. Already smoke had soared up the shafts and was asphyxiating people on the higher storeys.

Donn Arden left his room when he realized what was going on, but fortunately remembered to take his key with him. Many people who had been locked out were knocking on doors at random, begging to be admitted. He went to see how Bluebell was.

'We had about thirty people in her living-room, crying, bedraggled, smudged up, waiting for the ladders to come. But we were on the tenth floor,' he said. 'You didn't realize what was going on in any other part of the hotel. The loudspeakers were telling us to stay off the balconies — glass was falling, everything was dangerous — but you didn't realize the seriousness of the fire.'

Bluebell recalled becoming annoyed with him because he was walking around nervously waving his lighted cigarette about. 'I said, "Donn — put your cigarette out! There's enough smoke in this room already!"'

They stripped the bathroom of its towels and soaked them in all the water they could get out of the taps, then stuffed them under the door to stop the smoke coming in. When the taps ran dry they used the water in the flush toilet.

'Luckily,' said Donn Arden, 'I had been there a long time, and I had a very well-stocked bar — all kinds of mixes, tonic, soda water and loads of ice cubes. We had to use soda water to revive people — even the firemen when they came.'

Eventually a ladder long enough to reach the tenth floor was put against their balcony. Some twenty-six people were taken down it safely, the firemen using their skill to prevent those being rescued from becoming victims to vertigo.

Donn Arden continued: 'There was this one fat lady left who must have weighed about 300 lbs. There was no way she could have gone down the ladder, and we were wondering what on earth to do. Then this young fireman came in from the corridor; he could hardly breathe and was all smudged up, and nearly all in, so we tried to revive him. He saw that the woman was not going to get down the ladder, although Bluebell and I were prepared to go. So he said "Follow me" and took us out into the corridor. They had rigged up a cable with a sort of Christmas tree light every so many feet and we were told to hold on as we made our way along the corridor to the staircase, and we inched our way through the smoke and darkness and

The MGM Grand Hotel forty minutes after the fire started

Daughter Florence and Bluebell

dripping water until we had made it down to street level. And then I saw the fly loft of my theatre smoking and I was sick to the stomach. But we still didn't know how serious it was. We went across to a coffee shop, Denny's, across the street, and I said, "Blue — I don't want to go into the Dunes or the Aladdin with the show," as we sat gloomily and watched the theatre smoking.'

It was impossible to reach a telephone, and by the time Bluebell was able to call her son Patrick and daughter Florence, both of whom lived in Las Vegas, they turned out to be more hysterical than she was. No one in the Nevada city was unaware of the MGM disaster. The din of the warbling fire and ambulance sirens and the thrashing rotors of the helicopters hanging over the roof of the burning hotel were the chief sounds to be heard in Las Vegas that November morning.

'We later found that we had lost one of the ladies who was an assistant to the costume designer,' said Donn Arden. 'She was a fabulous worker, and she was also an early riser. She must have been on her way to the coffee shop or the basement so that she could get to the theatre and start getting shoes and hats ready for the kids who were rehearsing that day. They found her body in an elevator. Then there were two of my choreographers who had been celebrating in the bar on the twenty-third floor until 6 a.m. By sheer coincidence they had just seen a rerun of the movie *The Towering Inferno*, and they knew just what to do. They soaked the rugs and the bed

198

with the water from the bathroom, then got under them until the fireman came.'

The final death toll from the MGM Grand Hotel fire was eighty-four. But for the skill and heroism of the firefighters it might have been much higher, since nearly eight thousand people had been in the hotel at the time. By containing it, in spite of the conflagration in the casino, they had saved thousands of lives. It was fortunate, too, that the fire, which turned out to have been caused by a short circuit in the wiring in the ceiling of the Deli kitchen, had occurred at the time it did, and not when the casino, lobby and restaurants were busy, and that the winds were light that day, failing to fan the flames, and permitting helicopters to airlift guests from the roof to safety.

It was argued by apologists for the hotel's failure to alert its guests that the firemen's task would have been even harder had the alarm bells sounded, for they would have had the effect of driving more people into the smoke-filled hallways, where they would have suffocated. But the most damaging lack in the equipment of the lavish hotel was of sprinklers, which had not been required under the state building code in force at the time of its construction. The law was subsequently changed, and hard lessons were learned from the disaster.

While lawyers and insurers wrangled the management quickly and efficiently began the task of rebuilding the Grand Hotel. The charred, twisted debris was ripped out and the building bared for a full-scale refurbishment. Many of the 4,000 employees, including the dancers in the aborted *Jubilee* show, had to draw unemployment benefit or find temporary employment in other establishments while they waited for the new hotel to rise up out of the ashes. Donn Arden and Bluebell's schedules were busy as there was a new show, *Cocorico*, opening at the Lido in Paris, and they had to go back there to see it safely launched.

But Las Vegas has an extraordinary reputation for getting things done. On 29th July 1981 the MGM Grand Hotel re-opened, not merely fully restored to its pristine self, but with an additional eight-hundred-room extension, so that the place was literally bigger and better than ever before. The law to install sprinklers had been pushed through, and as if to reinforce its necessity, there had been another hotel fire that February at the Hilton, where eight people had died, and events had begun to match those of the preceding November. An arsonist was responsible.

The new MGM Grand Hotel is acutely conscious of fire safety. Every room is equipped with sprinklers, smoke detectors and speakers connected to a control room manned round the clock. There, in a room like something out of a science-fiction television series and sealed behind a firewall, a computer carries out constant checks of the system, and every part of the hotel can be monitored. Each guest on checking into his or her room is shown a short video in which Gene Kelly gives a rundown of the fire procedures. Millions of dollars have been spent to prevent a recurrence of the disaster.

Donn Arden's *Jubilee*, with its cast of 135, had its belated opening on 30th July, after two months of rehearsal in the restored Ziegfeld Room, which had new wiring, new seats, new furnishings, curtains, wall coverings, even dressing-room showers. It was not merely smoke and flame that had ruined the old theatre, but vast amounts of water. Next door, in the Celebrity Room, Dean Martin, an MGM perennial, was appearing again, while in the luxurious basement movie theatre an audience sank into luxurious armchairs, with cocktail waitresses in attendance, watching, appropriately, *Grand Hotel.*

In more than thirty years of mounting shows in Las Vegas, New York, Miami and Paris, Donn Arden, ironically, has often been associated with disasters, but he has usually staged them rather than suffered from them. The show at the Lido in Paris had a vivid re-enactment of the crash of the *Hindenburg*, the ill-fated Zeppelin which met its doom on arrival from Germany at Lakehurst, New Jersey in 1936, and in between the lavish numbers featuring bevies of outstandingly pretty girls with spectacular but limited clothing, the audience would gasp in horror as people would jump from the blazing replica of the airship, and by some stage magic their bodies would actually be engulfed in flames. In *Jubilee*, a show that is expected to run for ten years, he easily excels that particular diversion, firstly by staging a Samson and Delilah number, which naturally ends with the entire set disintegrating as the blinded hero demolishes the temple, toppling the columns together with a statue of a sacred bull, and then by a jolly shipboard sequence in which, after fun and games on deck, elegant couples dance in the grand salon of a luxury liner and watch a fashion show of exquisite lingerie, before the scene shifts to the boiler room, where sweating stokers are feeding the greedy furnaces, ogled from above by white-tied toffs and giggling girls in revealing evening dresses. But the ship is the *Titanic*, and the iceberg is subsequently struck. Water pours into the ship while everyone rushes for the lifeboats, and the final tableau shows the vessel, its lights still gleaming, sinking as laden lifeboats pull away from it.

It would be difficult to find a way of topping that, but the genius of Donn Arden prevails. The very next number is World War I, with topless girls marching into the trenches, and ancient biplanes popping out of the ceiling above the heads of the audience to circle each other in a dogfight. 'This is nothing,' he said, 'at Reno I've got a DC-9 with girls on the wings flying straight at the audience — scares the hell out of them!' The show at the MGM Grand Hotel, Reno, which, like that in Las Vegas, features Bluebell's dancers, is *Hello, Hollywood, Hello*, and is regarded by him as even more lavish than that in Las Vegas.

The experience of the Las Vegas fire was accepted by Bluebell as merely another event in a crowded life, and her survival as an indication that she

*Above: Bluebell demonstrates a step
and watches a rehearsal, right*

*Overleaf: a Lido line-up
in the early sixties*

Bluebell backstage at the Lido, 1966

was still good for many more years. Her children, meanwhile, were making their own lives, often in careers far removed from that of their mother. Bluebell's eldest child, Patrick, now lived in Las Vegas and had married an Australian girl, Tricia Lee, who was one of the principal dancers in the show. They had been immensely relieved to learn that she was safe.

Patrick was a medical student until his military service, and had originally intended to be a doctor. After his father's death he quit the university, with the intention of filling his shoes and helping Bluebell on the business side. Bluebell eventually decided that he would be better working in Las Vegas, and in 1974 he moved there, where the MGM Grand Hotel found that they could make use of his fluency in languages. He was interested in the stage, and eventually got a stage manager's job at the Dunes, but was forced to give it up when they closed their theatre room. Since then he has carved out a successful career in real estate.

His younger brother Francis followed Patrick into the Sorbonne, but studied law instead, and eventually joined the French civil service, where he works in a senior position in the agriculture ministry, from time to time producing mammoth and densely written reports on crop rotation. 'He is something of the eternal student,' says his mother. His sister Florence left her high school and joined the celebrated Paris fashion house of Yves St Laurent, interpreting for American buyers and making announcements at shows. Later she quit and went on a course studying eye exercising in Bordeaux, a developing branch of ophthalmic therapy. At the suggestion of her godfather, Frederic Apcar, who now lived in America, she emigrated, expecting the opportunities to be better there, and later married Mel Shapiro, who owned with his brother a chain of dry-cleaning establishments, and, being something of a Jewish comedian *manqué*, had made a name with his brilliantly sardonic television commercials for the firm. Florence, too, decided that rather than sit at home and be a housewife she would like to have a career, and also became a real estate negotiator. Las Vegas has a large semi-transient population, and the turnover in homes is relatively high, although competition between the many firms engaged in buying and selling houses tends to be fierce.

The youngest, Jean Paul, born in 1947, was less academically motivated than his siblings, and after schooldays trained to be a hairdresser, before going off to do his military service. He was not happy at returning to hairdressing, and instead decided to go to England. He then worked at the Curzon House Club in London as a croupier. Later he married an English girl and lived in Brighton, but later they divorced and he returned to France and now works for the Méridien hotel chain.

The Lido in Paris underwent a transformation in 1977. The Clerico brothers, Joseph and Louis, had opened it in 1946, and developed its world-famous reputation as a centre of Parisian night-time entertainment. But the premises had outgrown themselves, and the opportunity was taken to expand by moving to somewhere more spacious when the huge Normandie cinema, on the Champs-Elysées near the corner of the Rue Washington, was closed. A property consortium was formed with the intention of turning part of the building into a modern 'triple' — a cinema with three auditoriums — and the rest of the building into the new Lido. The intention was to create the largest and most luxurious night club in the world, capable of seating 1,200 diners, and with unparalleled stage facilities that were to include an ice rink, a pool, elevators, moveable platforms and a dressing-room area specially designed to cater for the nature of the show and the need for rapid changes of costume by the large cast. The construction took four years to accomplish.

Perhaps the most startling innovation was the sinking dining floor. The first impression that a visitor has when entering the Lido is that the stage area seems remarkably small, merely a dance floor, with an orchestra behind it, and that the sightlines for anyone not immediately in the front would be likely to be very poor. Then, as the moment of show time draws near each evening, the orchestra disappears, the floor is cleared, and suddenly the level part of the room begins to descend, the audience seated at their tables scarcely aware of the gentle movement. The dance floor is now a large projecting stage, and about to be the setting for a spectacular two-and-a-half-hour show, with an excellent view for everyone present, in spite of the immense size of the new Lido. A tiered crescent of tables forms a horseshoe around the performing area, and the elaborate chandeliers which have hitherto provided the lighting retract into the ceiling. Even without the consequent stage show the transformation from a restaurant with a dance floor into a cabaret theatre is an exciting spectacle, and provides a psychologically satisfying sense of anticipation that a mere dimming of the lights would scarcely achieve.

After forty years the Clericos are still associated with the Lido, and the family connection persists, with sons following their fathers. The Lido is open each night of the year, and on most of them many potential customers are turned away. A show is expected to last for four years, and the cost is such that it will require at least two years to reach break-even point even if the house is full for both performances every night. The only faint lull occurs shortly after Christmas, and traditionally this is the time when the old show closes and rehearsals begin for the new one, which then opens with a gala after it has been run in for two or three weeks and viewed by the press. The new show, which opened in 1985, replacing *Cocorico*, is called *Panache*, and is a further manifestation of the skills of René Fraday as the Lido's artistic director and Donn Arden as the director of the show, to say nothing of the artistry of the Italian costume designer, Folco, who himself has been working at the Lido for nearly thirty years.

Bluebell has four groups of dancers in the show, each under their own captain. They are the regular Bluebell Girls; the Bluebell Nude Dancers, who are the ones who appear topless; a new group called the Super Bluebells; and the Kelly Boy Dancers — a total of more than fifty performers. As always, the magnificent, tall, busty girls are the mainstay of the show, and all the dazzling and spectacular scenery and effects would be diminished were it not for their presence. A few years ago the Bluebells went topless, or at least some of them did, at their own insistence, both because they wished to earn more money and because they were proud of their bodies. Before the war there was strict demarcation between the Bluebells and the nudes at the Folies Bergère. But in the Eighties, when almost every French beach in the summer months is filled with young women sun-bathing without the top half of their bikinis — and indeed often without the bottom half either — there is little that is either shocking or provocative in the sight of the exposed female breast. Bluebell never forces a girl to bare herself if she does not want to, but if she does her breasts must be firm, round and attractive, not pendulous or minuscule, considerations which the girls readily accept.

The show is designed to blend movement, colour, music and light into a fast-paced, constantly-changing kaleidoscope, moving along at such a crisp pace that the passage of time goes unnoticed. After a brisk opening number comes a tribute to Broadway and Hollywood, including a rhythmic Fred and Ginger salute and 'Chantons sous la Pluie'. Then there's an ancient Egypt

206

The 1985 Lido show, due to end the Eighties

sequence, a winter sports number, a Polynesian spectacular (*Cocorico* had a fizzing jungle pool, elephants and threatened human sacrifice — *Panache* has an erupting volcano and a double waterfall), and the show nears its conclusion with '*Ça Va Jazzer!* [All that Jazz]', an excuse to entwine New Orleans minstrels, blues, jitterbug, big band swing and Chicago jazz into a whirlwind medley, before the finale. In between the big setpiece numbers are a succession of acrobats, singers, animal acts and other diversions to keep the audience distracted while waterfalls and volcanoes are quickly shoved into place behind the drapes. Every cue in the show is carefully met by constant practice and rehearsal, and some of the moving ramps and platforms depend on precise timing by the cast if the effect is to work properly. As the run of a show lengthens so does the experience of potential danger spots, when things can go wrong. The methods to cope with them are evolved pragmatically, although as Douglas Scott, for so many years the stage manager of the Lido, said, 'You always have to be ready for the unpredictable.' Rarely does the audience notice a missed cue, or a failed light, or a fumbled step, so polished is the presentation.

Panache is the latest entry in a long chronicle of theatrical history. The spirit of the show is that of the musical spectacles which have for more than a century been an integral element of entertainment in Paris. Although it may be a non-cerebral form of theatre, requiring no intellectual input on the part of either audience or performer, it is nevertheless not to be scorned. Such displays of music, dancing girls, tumblers and conjurers probably constitute the oldest form of entertainment there is, known to the civilizations of Greece and ancient Egypt, the Persians and the Mesopotamians. But it still goes on, and even when dressed up with radio mikes, amplifiers, lasers, electronically-controlled scene shifting and special effects, the essence is exactly the same, and every bit as honourable.

Bonsoir...   *A bientôt!*

15   Bluebells

THE LIFE OF a Bluebell girl is both exacting and exciting. Many start early, even as young as sixteen. Often they have been training as dancers since early childhood, with hopes set on the ballet, but then simply grew too tall. The Royal Ballet School at White Lodge, Richmond Park has produced many girls who were to go on to spend their careers in ostrich feathers and G-strings rather than tutus, but it is unlikely that much is made of that eventuality in the School's academic prospectus.

Quite often the thoroughly trained classical dancer must do some unlearning when she joins the Bluebells. There is a great difference between tapping in high heels bearing a heavy three-foot head-dress, and executing the conventional steps of classical ballet. But ballet-trained girls tend to have discipline, stamina and poise in abundance, three qualities very necessary to sustain a Bluebell career.

Bluebell regards a girl's personality as every bit as important as her dancing ability, and prefers those who can project a lively individuality. That would seem strange, given that when they are on stage in make-up and costumes it is immensely hard to tell one Bluebell from another; nevertheless she believes that the invisible characteristics are every bit as essential as the more obvious ones.

209

The eternal Bluebell Girl

Overleaf: a Lido jungle number

Peter Baker, Bluebell's manager for the United Kingdom, is her principal talent scout, and every year he interviews hundreds of applicants, many in their mid-teens. Often he will spot a potential Bluebell while she is still a schoolgirl, and hold her in reserve for a couple of years before she is ready to join the Paris company. But many of the dancers he recruits have already had professional experience, in clubs, theatre, television and elsewhere. It is a grotesquely overcrowded business, and competition is intense. The advertising columns of *The Stage* are closely scanned each week for announcements of auditions and usually dance directors have to spend much of their time weeding out scores of unsuitable applicants for every job.

Consequently, there is a certain amount of exploitation of young hopefuls who yearn for a stage career, and find that the only work they can get in the course of the year is a few summer weeks in a pier show at some lack-lustre minor seaside resort on a wage less than the prevailing unemployment benefit. But dim prospects do not deter thousands of girls from seeking a dancing career, and sometimes a rotten job is the only pathway to the acquisition of the precious Equity card, for membership of the stage trade union is an essential requirement, in Britain, at least.

Peter Baker does not merely wait for aspirant Bluebells to come to him. He keeps an eye on the dance schools and classes and sometimes invites promising dancers to audition, even if they had previously not considered the Bluebells. Miranda Coe, for example, a Ballet Rambert-trained dancer who had grown too tall for classical dancing, was recruited into the Bluebells, when Peter Baker saw her at her dance class and suggested that she audition the following day. Her subsequent career took her to Las Vegas for two years as well as Paris.

'The audition in front of Bluebell was relatively easy. What she was looking for was a reasonable amount of ballet training. The routine was easy — it wasn't like some where there are hundreds of people in the room, and you can never even see the routine. They were certainly looking for personality, for girls who would smile while they were dancing. Then we had a chat with Bluebell — I think she makes her mind up very quickly when she meets us.'

Nicola Harvey, who was then Nicky Jones, another ex-Bluebell who later became an executive for British Film Year, recalls how she was hired after working as a model. She had spent five years studying ballet as a little girl, but had later dropped it. She had a flatmate who was seeing Bluebell at the Dance Centre for a Las Vegas audition, and she went along with her, but merely to attend class. But she was introduced to Bluebell, who asked her if she could dance. 'I was about to say "You must be joking!" when my friend, who was very ambitious for me, said, "Does she *dance*! That girl could kick up a storm!" So I found myself in an audition with all these very professional girls doing *grands jetés* and *grands battements*, but somehow I got through, and was asked to go to Paris. I was a lousy model, anyway!'

A few days later she arrived in Paris and, not quite knowing what to do, took a taxi to Bluebell's flat in the Rue de la Faisanderie. Bluebell was still asleep and the maid admitted her. After an hour's wait Bluebell took her to the Lido, by Métro, including the change at Place Charles de Gaulle, as she clutched her suitcases, and dumped her in a rehearsal. 'I took one look at all these girls in legwarmers and leotards with their legs behind their ears and I wanted to run out. But Miss Bluebell is very authoritative — you do what she says.'

She was twenty-four at the time, a relatively mature age for a new Bluebell. The younger ones, some of whom may never have been abroad before, are greatly dependent on Bluebell's kind but firm attitude. She believes in breaking them in quickly. Within hours of arrival they are rehearsing parts of the show, and are quite likely to be actually appearing in it within three days. The nature of the Lido show is such that it can be learned in bits rather than as a whole, and there are routines eminently suitable to enable new girls to get the feel of the performance and the audience. Usually on their first night, once they have got their accommodation sorted out, which is no easy matter in view of the crowded market in Paris apartments, they sit through the entire show at a special table, markedly not plied with champagne and smoked salmon.

Almost every afternoon there are rehearsals at the Lido. The vast room with the worklights on looks about as glamorous as an aircraft hangar. Dancers in many permutations of rehearsal leotards go through their routines to an amplified taped playback. A new girl usually has an experienced Bluebell assigned to look after her, not merely to show her the steps, but to fill her in on the unwritten rules, the etiquette of Bluebelldom. In some respects it must be very like the initiation period at a new school. You never argue with Miss Bluebell, you never run off the stage in the middle of a rehearsal, you always look your best when you are going to or from the Lido. For some the strain is great, and there are sometimes tearful cries for help, anguished phone calls to parents and occasional outright defections. The first few days, rather like joining the army, are undoubtedly the worst, but Bluebell knows that once that early period is over most of the new recruits, if her hunches have been correct, will settle in and enjoy it. Very rarely does she make a mistake and have to send a hopelessly neurotic girl home after the settling-in period.

Most of the nightly Lido audiences is made up of tourists — with Japanese, Germans and Americans predominating. 'Some of them are so tired that they fall asleep, and put napkins over their heads — I could never understand how they could do that when we were dancing only a few feet away. It's often a very strange audience,' said Miranda Coe.

The backstage area is not spacious but well-planned, although every inch of space counts and during showtime nothing can be out of place. Some of the changes are very rapid, and costumes hang where they can be quickly grabbed and donned in the correct sequence. Before curtain up the girls must get themselves made-up, a task which the older hands can accomplish in a phenomenally short time. Bluebells are very careful when they sunbathe, because the application of all-over body make-up on a reddened skin is not only painful but can result in a streaky effect. Bluebell tends to prefer a porcelain look to a vivid suntan, and will be quite scathing if a girl comes back from holiday several shades darker than when she went away. The means by which body make-up is applied is a large and very ordinary car sponge, which can cover a wide area of flesh very quickly. It takes about fifteen minutes to put on.

Tanya Spencer, now one of Bluebell's captains, described how some of the girls on arrival would warm up to get the muscles in trim before putting their make-up on, while others would go straight to the bathroom. 'There is only room for two or three girls at a time, so the time spent there is very limited. Occasionally people come up with ideas like paint rollers or sprays, but the sponge is best. When you've got that coat on you feel quite dressed, it's like a second skin.'

At the next stage of preparation the facial make-up is tidied up and the hair is put in place. Then tights are pulled on and the precious G-string. They stay in place no matter what costume changes are required. For some reason the girls are responsible for their own G-strings, and usually make them themselves. Since so little material is required the cost is hardly exorbitant. They also have to buy their own make-up, and although there are individual variations to suit personal colourings, they have to conform generally to the uniform look. Their flesh-toned fishnet tights are carefully looked after, as they are expected to last. Holes must be carefully darned on a mushroom, and are frequent occurrences during performances. 'We used to get the principals to pass theirs down to us,' said Nicola Harvey. 'They were better quality with more stretch, and less likely to go baggy at the ankles, which was always a big problem.'

The shoes and costume for the opening comes next. Shoes, like tights, usually stay on throughout the show, and have to be hard-wearing. The first thing to wear out is not the sole, nor the upper, but the strap. But usually one pair of shoes should last, with an occasional repair, for two years.

There are dressers to help the girls, and to ensure that everything is ready on cue. One of the worst back-stage crimes is for someone to take part of someone else's costume, particularly an item such as a hat, which has a particular fit. 'You have to go on whatever happens,' says Miranda Coe. 'There's usually so much happening on the stage that the audience doesn't usually notice anything amiss. But Bluebell does — she will always be aware of a gap or something wrong, and it is best to go to her and tell her before she comes to you.'

Bluebell occupies a tiny dressing-room with the number '13' on the door and there she receives her captains. To the staff at the Lido she is always referred to as 'Miss', which to English ears seems to heighten the schoolmistress image. The girls would never dream of calling her 'Bluebell' to her face, it is always prefaced with the respectful title. At some stage she walks round the dressing area saying good evening to each of the girls, who will be resting or limbering up for the performance. Sometimes she might take one of them aside and ask about her weight problem or some other factor that may be affecting her performance, but she does it discreetly and privately. Little, however, escapes her. The private lives of the girls at the Lido may be very different from the cloistered state in which she found herself when she was in the line more than fifty years ago, but the basic psychology remains the same and she is very aware of it. She must be both headmistress and surrogate mother.

Weight is a serious consideration, particularly among the younger Bluebells who are undergoing the puppy-fat phase, and on rare occasions a girl has to be sent home until she has lost perhaps a stone, when she can apply to return. The plump dancing girls of the Twenties and Thirties, with their heavy thighs and thick waists, would be laughed off the stage nowadays, and Bluebell, who in those days was more full-figured than she is now, regards it as ironic that old-fashioned voluptuousness of a time when half the population was on or near the breadline has been replaced by the stringy athletic look favoured in the more prosperous Eighties. Most of the girls go to dance class two, three or even five times a week, not just to keep their dancing up to standard but also to preserve their shapes, as if two shows each night was insufficient to do the job.

Once the show has started, at 10.30, there is little time for rest as it continues at a relentless rate. One of the biggest potential hazards is the possibility of dancers colliding with one another as they run offstage to change their costumes, and as far as possible a 'one-way' system is in force in the long dressing-room that runs behind the stage. Some changes are down to a mere forty-five seconds, which calls for great precision. The only pauses in the show come when the speciality acts go on in front of the curtain, giving valuable time for the stagehands to set things up for the most spectacular numbers.

'It's really a show for looking at,' says Miranda Coe, 'not for thinking about, not for laughs. But it can be enjoyable if you are in the right mood.'

Although it would be disingenuous to suggest that given the presence of such a large number of attractive young women, a large number of whom expose their breasts, the show does not have erotic overtones, it is a very wholesome spectacle that should not disturb even the most strait-laced grandmother. Parents of Bluebells who have visited the Lido for the first time, apprehensive at the thought of witnessing their daughters' topless display, have been enchanted by the show. 'You only feel naked,' said one Bluebell, 'if you are not wearing any body make-up.'

Nicola Harvey had the strange experience in her post-Bluebell career of attending a meeting of feminists who were shown a video on the exploitation of women; one sequence included the Bluebells. She realized that at any moment her own face would be visible, as well as a large part of her body not concealed by feathers, rhinestones and fishnets. In fact nobody recognized her; but when the lights went up she told her colleagues that she had been a Bluebell, and was in that very sequence. 'As far as I was concerned the only people being exploited were those willing to pay through the nose to watch us. I suppose they enjoyed it. I never met a Bluebell who thought that her womanhood was being exploited, just because she had a good body.' She was then questioned with great interest by the ladies about life with the Bluebells, she felt not without a certain amount of envy.

There is a brief interval at the Lido between the two shows in which the waiters perform a nightly miracle of ushering one audience out, whisking off and replacing the tablecloths, and resetting the places in readiness for the next. Backstage there is a mere half-hour to take things easy before it all begins again. The second show literally moves even faster because its running time is shorter, some of the extraneous acts having been taken out. When it is all over, there is a rush for the showers so that the body make-up can be removed — generally with warm water and plenty of liquid soap. Taxis are laid on to take the girls home, but some prefer to unwind by going

The intimate atmosphere of the old Lido

off to have a meal first, there being a number of restaurants in the area that keep open most of the night.

Because of the strange hours that the girls work it is extremely difficult for them to acquire boy friends, unless they too work to the same eccentric pattern. Few men would find it easy to adjust to a relationship where the girl came home between 3.30 and 4 a.m. every night. Consequently it is among those with similar lifestyles that relationships are formed, particularly the Lido waiters, many of who have been or are temporarily 'resting' performers themselves.

A large number of the girls from England fail to become proficient in French, particularly if they share their apartments with other English-speaking girls and do not have French boy friends. As much English is heard backstage at the Lido as French, and so the incentives are lacking. Occasionally linguistic shortcomings can cause problems, and Bluebell's secretary is used to anguished calls from the girls for assistance in sorting out some mundane domestic problem, such as an exorbitant gas bill which must be queried with the authorities. The girls work very hard, six nights a week, and sometimes seven when they are deputizing for an absentee. But

Bluebell, in her 70s, performs a party number

the time passes very quickly for them. After a year or two's experience at the Lido they are likely to be asked by Bluebell to go to Las Vegas or Reno, or join one of the touring companies. Las Vegas is usually a popular posting — as far away from home as Nevada a girl can feel really independent and not within easy reach of anxious parents, and the salary is good and the living expenses low, enabling money to be saved for the future. The life of a practising Bluebell is a short one, and few stay as long as their thirtieth birthdays, unless they have achieved promotion to captain.

Over the years there have been around 14,000 Bluebells, and a surprisingly large number of them send Bluebell cards at Christmas-time. Just as a distinguished headmistress could lay claim to remember the faces of all her former pupils, so Bluebell manages to recall almost everyone she has employed. She makes a point of knowing the names of the five hundred or so current members of all her troupes in Paris, Las Vegas, Reno and on tour. Ex-Bluebells are proud of belonging to an exclusive band, and when a batch of them get together they behave like reunited schoolgirls. Some, those who were with her at the Folies Bergère, are as old as Bluebell herself. They all, young or old, tend to look back on their time with her as a highpoint of their lives, just like men who served in a crack regiment.

Bluebell has, with the passing time, become regarded as a show-business legend. She has had the experience of being the subject of the mushy television programme *This is Your Life*, with the compere, Eamonn

Andrews, surprising her in the middle of a Lido rehearsal, and dragging her off to a nearby studio where old Bluebells, ex-inmates of Besançon, and her far-flung family were reunited. The Variety Club of Great Britain honoured her with a gala luncheon at the Savoy, commemorating the fiftieth anniversary of the Bluebells, with Ken Dodd, the Liverpool comedian whose shows at Blackpool and the London Palladium had featured the girls, Sir Anton Dolin, one of her oldest friends and supporters, and Barry Cryer, the comedian and scriptwriter, and with the Chief Barker, Tom Nicholas, presenting her with a mounted silver heart, the symbol of the club, whose object is to raise money for children's charities. Several of the girls flew over from Paris with her to attend the function, and greeted arriving guests in their costumes, causing heads to turn and cameras to click. She has been personally involved in many charities herself, and the Bluebells have raised hundreds of thousands of pounds with special appearances.

Honours have also come her way in France, her home for more than half a century. In 1984 she was awarded the Paris Medal of Honour in a ceremony at the Hôtel de Ville, and the citation referred not only to her generous support for the sick and injured, but for her 'inestimable contribution to the enchantment of Paris nights'.

Pierre Louis-Guérin and Bluebell

Postscript

IN 1981 MISS BLUEBELL and her dancers made the cover of *The Sunday Times Magazine*, a measure of the shift in public taste that was now prepared to take her contribution to the world of performing arts seriously. This was followed by appearances on television in talk shows, notably *Parkinson*, and her story became better known. But the most significant manifestation of the new interest in her remarkable life came when a distinguished freelance television producer, Richard Bates, who had been responsible for many successful drama series such as *The Avengers* and *The Prime of Miss Jean Brodie*, decided that Bluebell's career could form the basis of a television serial.

The years from the time she left Liverpool and Mary Murphy to join the Hot Jocks until the end of the war and the beginnings of the post-war Bluebells at the Lido were to be the basis for the programmes, a time span that encompassed the years as a Jackson girl, the periods at the Folies Bergère and the Paramount, her marriage to Marcel, the start of the war and her subsequent internment at Besançon, as well as Marcel's incarceration and escape from Gurs, the liberation and finally the picking up of the pieces that were shattered in 1939.

For a producer Bluebell's story is a gift — an indomitable woman pitted

Left: Carolyn Pickles and Bluebell. Above Thelma Ruby plays Mistinguett for the BBC

against heavy odds and winning through, but set against a glamorous show business background that would provide colour, spectacle, stars and excitement. Richard Bates was determined that his series should be produced with a high level of integrity, and he carefully selected his team. The scripts for the eight episodes were written by Paul Wheeler, a television and film writer with an enviable list of credits. The director was to be Moira Armstrong, one of the best working in Britain, and to Richard Bates' delight the BBC were excited by the idea, deciding to make *Bluebell* their major drama serial for the winter of 1986.

In the autumn of 1984 Richard Bates, now the executive producer, together with Moira Armstrong; Brian Spiby, her producer; the designers Chris Pemsel and Jan Spoczynski; the costume designers Verity Lewis and Janet Powell; and various other key members of the production staff, arrived in Paris to begin the extensive process of pre-production that would enable the series to go before the cameras in the late spring of the following year. Bluebell received the horde in her flat and faced a barrage of questions from the youngest member of the team, Sophie Neville, who was chief researcher as well as floor assistant.

The next big test was to find an actress capable of playing the leading

Carolyn Pickles as Miss Bluebell and 1939 Folies number restaged

role. It was not an easy task — she had to be a good dancer, yet primarily an actress. But it was the kind of part that could create a new star. After extensive auditions Carolyn Pickles was chosen. She had danced as a teenager, but now at thirty was obliged to take up extensive classes to regain her skills. However, she had the right kind of blonde good looks, the characteristic firmness of jaw and the effervescent vitality needed to portray the younger Bluebell, as well as the acting skill to enable her in the course of the drama to put on years, from the teenager of the Hot Jocks to the mature woman at the end of the war.

Other casting was also fortunate. The small but immensely effective role of Mistinguett was given to Thelma Ruby, a celebrated star of West End revues in the Fifties who had after her marriage spent many years living in Israel, and therefore out of the public eye. She applied herself to studying the Mistinguett technique, watching over and again fragments of suriving film footage, and in delivering the old songs managed to capture something of the humorous flirtation with the audience that made her a superstar of the French music hall and revue. It was also necessary to flash her legs in the approved Mistinguett manner — a sudden hiking up of the sequinned evening dress — but all agreed they were in good shape. The part of Bluebell's musician husband, Marcel, was played by a fine actor, Philip Sayer, and Peter Reeves provided a proficient interpretation of Maurice Chevalier.

But perhaps the most ambitious aspect of the BBC serial lay in the superbly produced ensemble numbers choreographed by Anthony Van Laast, which re-created the style of the Jackson Girls in Berlin, the pre-war Folies Bergère and the Paramount shows. A large, recently-closed art deco cinema in Grays, Essex was transformed into the Paramount, Paris. The huge stage of the Scala, Berlin, was fashioned from a theatre in Harrogate, and the Folies Bergère itself was the Civic Theatre, Halifax, which with the addition of panelling, boxes and new seating in the auditorium looked convincingly like Paul Derval's theatre in the Thirties. Carolyn Pickles is a Halifax girl, a member of the same proud Yorkshire family which produced the famous broadcaster and comedian Wilfred Pickles, and the choice of her hometown was particularly happy.

It was to Halifax that Bluebell herself came to watch the shooting. On stage the girls with their turquoise ostrich feathers were performing an intricate routine against a steep, glittering staircase with nudes standing in various niches in true Folies style. The dimensions of the shallow Folies stage had been followed, even though there was actually more space to spare, and the staircase looked like an invitation to disaster with its acute but historically accurate pitch. For the girls the tension was twofold, not just to get the steps right without falling headlong down the stairs, but to pass muster with Bluebell herself, now decidedly a living legend, especially as one or two of the dancers the BBC had recruited had once actually been

Rehearsing for the BBC drama series Bluebell

Bluebells, and had not concealed from the other girls her reputation for high standards.

They need not have worried. Bluebell walked into a special box in the theatre, sat down, heard Marcel's music start up and saw the girls moving down the staircase in their head-dresses and feathers, watched by an audience of Leeds extras attired in Thirties-style dinner jackets and evening gowns. For a moment it seemed as if the past had miraculously been brought to life. Bluebell beamed and happily sighed, 'This is what it's all about!'